Quiet Girl SZN

THIS JOURNAL BELONGS TO:

_____

Quiet Girls SZN- 90 Day Lessons for your Soul

© 2024 Towanda McEachern

All rights reserved. No part of this publication may be reproduced, distributed, or transmitted in any form or by any means, including photocopying, recording, or other electronic or mechanical methods, without the prior written permission of the publisher, except in the case of brief quotations embodied in critical reviews and certain other noncommercial uses permitted by copyright law. For permission requests, please contact the publisher at the address below.

www.aliferecycled.com

ISBN: 979-8-9915060-0-7
Printed in the United States of America

Unless otherwise noted, all scripture quotations are taken from the Holy Bible, New International Version®, NIV®. Copyright © 1973, 1978, 1984, 2011 by Biblica, Inc.® Used by permission. All rights reserved worldwide.

Scripture References Section:

All scripture references in this devotional are from the New International Version (NIV) unless otherwise indicated. The NIV Bible is used to provide clarity and understanding in a modern-day context, perfect for diving deeper into God's Word. The translation was carefully selected to ensure the messages are relevant and relatable for today's women as they seek to discover their self-worth and confidently live out their purpose in Christ.

This Book is dedicate to memory of my dear sister
"Natasha "Tabitha" Sharon Carruthers
Rest in Peace my love

Writing is no easy feat, for all the things I am able to accomplish, I do so because of the love and support of my family.

To my husband Roger, thank you for being patient with me while I figure out this life God has called me to live. Thank you for enduring all my late night hours writing this and all the other ideas I come up with. I am grateful for the love and growth we have shared over our many years together,

To my youngest daughter Kayla, thank you for sharing me with others. I pray you allow God to use your life for His Glory. Thank you for all the lessons you have taught me.

To my oldest daughter Kari, thank you for pushing and inspiring me. Thank you for designing the layout and for encouraging me on those days when things weren't going the way I wanted them to. Thank you for the push.

Quiet Girl SZN: An Invitation to Stillness

Quiet Girl SZN was born from a season in my life when I found myself constantly running ahead of God. I wasn't taking the time to sit quietly and listen to all the instructions He had for me. The moment an idea came to mind, I'd rush forward, confident in my talents and gifts. For years, I relied on these gifts that God had graciously given me, thinking they were enough to carry me through. But eventually, I realized something important: moving without the One who gave the gift can only take you so far.

I reached a point where I felt frustrated and exhausted, despite all my efforts. That's when I recognized I had been moving in my own strength, not His. I was reminded of the scripture in Isaiah: "They that wait upon the Lord shall renew their strength; they shall mount up with wings as eagles, they shall run and not grow weary, they shall walk and not faint." This truth became the foundation of my journey toward learning to rest and wait on God.

In those moments of rest, God began to reveal important things. First, He revealed me to myself—showing me who I truly am. Second, He revealed the plans He has for my life, reminding me that His plans are far greater than my own. And third, He revealed the people around me, helping me discern who was for me and who was not.

Quiet Girl SZN is about more than just being silent. It's about intentionally seeking God and creating space for Him to speak. For me, it started by waking up early in the morning before the world stirred. At 5:00 a.m., I would make tea, light a candle, and sit with God. With instrumental music playing softly in the background and scripture gently displayed on the screen, I would simply sit in His presence.

At first, it was uncomfortable—I was so used to bringing God my lists of wants and needs. But slowly, I began to realize that it wasn't about me telling God what to do, but about me being still so I could hear what He wanted me to do., I resisted the idea of waking up so early, thinking it was too much of a sacrifice. But as I surrendered to God's call, I began to see the beauty in those quiet moments.

Tragedy also shaped this season for me, as the sudden loss of my sister Natasha shifted my perspective on life and purpose. In the midst of grief, I answered the call to meet with God every morning, and He met me there, even in the silence and tears.

This devotional was born out of those still, quiet moments—moments when God revealed deep truths and spoke to my heart. I pray that as you journey through these pages, you too will experience the power of intentional quiet time with God. May He reveal who you are, what He's called you to do, and who is truly for you. And remember, if God is for you, that's more than enough.

You are More than ENOUGH

Table of CONTENTS

- DAY 1 - HAVE A SEAT
- DAY 2 - SLOW DOWN
- DAY 3 - YOU ARE WORTHY
- DAY 4 - WALK YOUR WALK
- DAY 5 - THAT GIRL TALENTED
- DAY 6 - BE YOU
- DAY 7 - WHO'S "WILL" DO YOU WANT?
- DAY 8 - I GOT QUESTIONS SIS!
- DAY 9 - TAP IN
- DAY 10 - EMBRACING PURPOSE
- DAY 11 - I SEE YOU SIS
- DAY 12 - DON'T BE SCARED
- DAY 13 - YOU BETTER THANK GOD
- DAY 14 - CHECK YOUR CIRCLE
- DAY 15 - REST YOUR SOUL
- DAY 16 - DO YOU RECOGNIZE HIS VOICE?
- DAY 17 - YOU BETTER CELEBRATE
- DAY 18 - I DON'T DOUBT IT
- DAY 19 - HE IS YOUR STRENGTH
- DAY 20 - DON'T BE BITTER
- DAY 21 - WATCH YOUR MOUTH
- DAY 22 - BE PATIENT
- DAY 23 - RELAX YOU ARE ON A JOURNEY
- DAY 24 - ITS OK TO CHANGE YOUR MIND
- DAY 25 - I'M PRAYING FOR YOU

GIRL, GET READY

- DAY 26 - LISTEN
- DAY 27 - YOU BETTER ASK
- DAY 28 - PAY ATTENTION
- DAY 29 - JUST SAY YES
- DAY 30 - THE ILLUSION OF CONTROL
- DAY 31 - YOU ARE CONSISTENT
- DAY 32 - TAKE SOMETHING OFF YOUR PLATE
- DAY 33 - WHAT IS YOUR LIFE FOR?
- DAY 34 - STOP WASTING TIME
- DAY 35 - IT'S TIME YOU MAKE A MOVE
- DAY 36 - GET OUT OF YOUR WAY
- DAY 37 - PREPARE FOR WHAT YOU WANT
- DAY 38 - BELIEVE IN YOURSELF
- DAY 39 - ENCOURAGE YOURSELF
- DAY 40 - DON'T BE A QUITTER
- DAY 41 - FOCUS!
- DAY 42 - WHAT'S YOUR MOTIVE?
- DAY 43 - TAKE A MOMENT TO REFLECT
- DAY 44 - REKINDLE THAT DREAM
- DAY 45 - KEEP YOUR EYES ON GOD
- DAY 46 - EMBRACE THE NEW VERSION OF YOU
- DAY 47 - JUMP!
- DAY 48 - YOU ARE A GIFT
- DAY 49 - PRAYER CHANGES THINGS
- DAY 50 - STOP THE SABOTAGE

GIRL, GET READY

- DAY 51 - EVERYTHING DON'T HAVE TO BE HARD
- DAY 52 - STEAL AWAY
- DAY 53 - STOP DREAMING AND START DOING
- DAY 54 - STOP BEING SO BUSY
- DAY 55 - ARE YOU MAKING AN IMPACT?
- DAY 56 - DON'T MAKE A DECISION ALONE
- DAY 57 - IT MAY BE A TRUST THING
- DAY 58 - PICK UP A BOOK
- DAY 59 - LEAD WITH LOVE
- DAY 60 - DO YOU DREAM
- DAY 61 - ARE YOU GROWING?
- DAY 62 - DON'T CHASE THE WRONG THING
- DAY 63 - IT'S NOT ALWAYS ABOUT YOU
- DAY 64 - IT'S UP TO YOU
- DAY 65 - WHERE YOU AT?
- DAY 66 - IT'S TIME TO GET CLEAR
- DAY 67 - CONFRONT YOUR FEARS
- DAY 68 - ARE YOU FEELING STUCK?
- DAY 69 - YOU MUST FORGIVE
- DAY 70 - GREATER IS COMING
- DAY 71 - IT COULD BE A SET UP
- DAY 72 - DON'T WORRY
- DAY 73 - THIS HAS TO STOP
- DAY 74 - YOUR PAIN WASN'T FOR NOTHING
- DAY 75 - STOP BEING ALL OVER THE PLACE

- DAY 76 - YOU GOT THIS
- DAY 77 - SHARE YOUR STORY
- DAY 78 - STOP SETTLING
- DAY 79 - YOU ARE WORTHY
- DAY 80 - CHANGE YOUR MIND
- DAY 81 - JUST TRUST GOD
- DAY 82 - WHAT ARE YOU PASSIONATE ABOUT
- DAY 83 - WHAT'S EATING YOU?
- DAY 84 - YOU MAY NEED TO WALK AWAY
- DAY 85 - YOU ARE GOING TO BE ALRIGHT
- DAY 86 - DON'T RUN AHEAD OF GOD
- DAY 87 - HOLD ON
- DAY 88 - BE QUIET
- DAY 89 - IT'S YOUR RESPONSIBLE
- DAY 90 - GIRL, LET'S CELEBRATE

DAY 01

GIRL, HAVE A SEAT

Did you know there is much peace in spending quiet time with God? It's where you truly get an opportunity to know yourself and to be in His presence. In those quiet moments, you can truly hear from Him—without distractions, without noise, just stillness. So often, our minds are filled with thoughts about what we want to do, what we need to do, and how we need to do it. We are constantly planning, organizing, and strategizing. But there are moments when God simply wants us to rest in Him, and there is such peace in realizing that you don't always have to be in control of everything.

"Be still, and know that I am God."
Psalm 46:10a (NIV)

In the stillness, God speaks. When you allow Him to work in your life during the quiet moments, He gives you instruction, direction, and reassurance. That is where true peace ultimately comes in—not because you've figured everything out, but because you've trusted God to guide you. Instead of living in the overwhelm of life, in constant motion, God invites us to slow down and rest in His presence. When we do, we are able to see life with clearer vision and a renewed sense of purpose.

It's in solitude that you gain a deeper understanding of who you are, what life means, and what God desires to speak into your heart. The world tells us to go, go, go, but God says, "Be still." In that stillness, you are reminded of His sovereignty, His love, and His perfect plan for your life. You don't have to figure it all out—God is already working on your behalf.

QUIET GIRL SZN

QUIET TIME

Take a few moments today to sit in silence before God. What is He saying to you in the quiet? How can you surrender control and trust Him more in your daily life?

PRAYER

Dear Lord, thank You for the gift of quiet moments where I can be still in your presence. Help me to quiet my mind and listen for your voice. Give me peace as I release my need to control everything and trust in Your perfect plan. Show me the path You want me to take, and guide me with Your wisdom. In Jesus' name, Amen.

DAY 02

GIRL, SLOW DOWN

Sometimes, when you're moving so fast, you can't see what you need to do. It's easy to get caught up in the hustle and bustle of life, jumping from one task to the next, feeling productive, yet never really stopping to assess what's truly important. You may find yourself busy all the time, but being busy doesn't always mean you're being effective. There is great power in slowing down and seeking God's direction for your life.

Slowing down gives you the space to gain clarity and perspective. It allows you to step back and see things for what they truly are, not just how they appear in the moment. Sometimes, the things you think are important lose significance when viewed through the lens of God's eternal purpose. But if you're constantly on the move, never taking the time to pause and connect with God, you may miss the opportunity to receive His wisdom and guidance.

> *"In repentance and rest is your salvation, in quietness and trust is your strength."*
> *Isaiah 30:15a (NIV)*

There is immense power in stillness. When you take the time to rest in God's presence and listen for His voice, you will find strength, peace, and direction. The world may tell you to keep pushing, to do more, and to never stop, but God invites you to pause and let Him lead. In the quiet moments, when you allow your soul to be still, He can reveal His will for your life in ways that you couldn't see when you were constantly in motion.

Slowing down is not about doing less—it's about making space for what truly matters. It's about giving God room to guide you in the right direction, so you don't spend your energy chasing things that don't align with His plan for you. When you slow down, you can reflect on your life, seek God's wisdom, and make decisions that lead you closer to the purpose He has for you.

QUIET GIRL SZN

QUIET TIME

Take a few moments to pause today. In the stillness, ask yourself: Am I moving so fast that I'm missing God's direction for my life? What areas of my life do I need to surrender to God, trusting Him to guide my steps?

PRAYER

Lord please help me slow down and seek Your direction for my life. Help me to prioritize what truly matters and to hear your voice in the quiet moments. Guide me with your wisdom and help me trust that you are working everything out for my good. I surrender my busyness and ask that You lead me on the path You have prepared for me. In Jesus' name, Amen.

DAY 03

GIRL, YOU ARE WORTHY

The world will try to tell you who you are. You'll see it on social media, in comparison to others' lives, in society's definition of success, beauty, and value. As you scroll through the highlights of someone else's life, it's easy to start measuring yourself, wondering where you fit in and whether you're good enough. But your value isn't found in any of these places. Your true worth is in the fact that God created you, and when He did, He knew exactly what He was doing. God formed you with intention, love, and purpose.

> "I praise you because I am fearfully and wonderfully made; your works are wonderful, I know that full well."
> Psalm 139:14 (NIV)

When you see yourself through God's eyes, you begin to focus less on what the world considers your flaws and more on the masterpiece that He carefully designed. You are fearfully and wonderfully made—full of value, worth, and purpose. Even in moments of doubt, pain, or trauma, God's love for you remains unchanged. You may struggle at times to see your own worth, but God's love is a constant reminder that you are needed, you are cherished, and your life has meaning.

Your past does not diminish your worth, and your mistakes do not define your value. God has called you for a reason, and He sees the beauty, strength, and potential in you. No matter where you've been, what you've done, or what you've gone through, know that your life is precious to Him. You are worthy, and your existence has purpose beyond what the world says.

QUIET GIRL SZN

QUIET TIME

Take some time today to reflect on how God sees you. What are the truths He speaks over your life? Ask Him to reveal to you the areas where you need to embrace your worth and let go of comparison.

PRAYER

Lord, thank You for creating me with purpose and value. Help me to see myself through Your eyes and to remember that my worth is not defined by the world but by You. Teach me to love myself as You love me and to embrace the purpose You have for my life. In Jesus' name, Amen.

DAY 04

GIRL, WALK YOUR WALK

Confidence may not be something that you just wake up with. Truth be told, there are times when you don't always feel so confident. Life has a way of throwing challenges your way, making you question your ability to handle them. But having a relationship with God and understanding who you are, why you are here, and why you've been created will help give you the confidence and boldness to walk in the authority you have been given for your assignment. Confidence grows when you are deeply rooted in God's truth and promises, and when you know that your worth comes from Him and not from the world's standards.

Walking with God helps to ensure that you are being guided by His hand. When you rely on Him, your confidence is not dependent on circumstances or external validation but on the assurance that He is walking alongside you every step of the way. It's about knowing that you are never alone, and no matter what you face, He is there to strengthen you, guide you, and equip you for everything that lies ahead.

> "I can do all this through him who gives me strength." Philippians 4:13 (NIV)

Look at your life through the lens of how God sees you, and you will see what a beautiful life you get to live and how you can walk it out boldly knowing that He is with you every step of the way. Walking in confidence and boldness changes your perspective on how you view things. It changes how you enter into rooms, especially rooms you don't feel qualified to enter. You belong in every room you enter. When you enter, be sure to enter with God, confidence, boldness, and grace. When you trust in God's plans for your life, you can stand firm, knowing that He will carry you through the challenges with strength and purpose.

QUIET TIME

Reflect on how you see yourself. Are you showing up with confidence, boldness, and grace? What steps can you take to invite more of God's truth into your life so that you can walk in the fullness of who He has called you to be?

PRAYER

God, help me to be the woman You have called me to be and to show up confidently, boldly, and gracefully. Remind me daily that my strength comes from You and that I can do all things through Your power. In Jesus' name, Amen.

DAY 05

GIRL, YOU GOT TALENT

Have you ever received a gift? Of course you have. Have you ever received a "just-because" gift? Those are the best gifts; it's not your birthday, Christmas, or any special occasion, but simply because someone thought about you. These kinds of gifts are unexpected and filled with love, and they leave a lasting impact on us.

It is the same with our gifts and talents that God has given us. God, in His infinite wisdom, has blessed each of us with unique gifts, and the most interesting part about gifts is that you don't work for them. You don't have to earn them—they are freely given by His grace. Some of us are blessed with multiple gifts, and even though those gifts belong to us, they are not for us alone. They are meant to be used to serve others. We are God's hands and feet on this earth, and through our gifts and talents, we have the opportunity to make a difference, to bless, and to uplift those around us.

> *"Each of you should use whatever gift you have received to serve others, as faithful stewards of God's grace in its various forms." 1 Peter 4:10 (NIV)*

Sometimes we discount the things that come to us too easily. Have you ever had someone tell you, "Oh, you're so great at that," and you reply, "Oh, girl, that's nothing"? But actually, it is something! That thing you do effortlessly is a gift, and it's special. If we start to recognize the beauty and value in the gifts God has given us and lean into them, we would move differently in our lives. We would start to live with more purpose and intention. Once you embrace and recognize the gift you have been given, you can start to use it for God's glory, touching lives, and spreading His love in ways that only you can.

QUIET TIME

Take a moment to reflect. Have you recognized and accepted the gifts God has given you? How are you using them to serve others?

PRAYER

God, help me to recognize and embrace the gifts You have given me. Show me how to use them to serve others and to bring glory to Your name. Guide me as I seek to be a faithful steward of Your grace. In Jesus' name, Amen.

DAY 06

GIRL, BE YOU

Living authentically is the freedom of being yourself without comparison. It's easy to get caught up in comparing yourself to others - the way they look, walk, talk, think, their job, their home, how much money they have. Their marriage may seem happy and healthy and all their kids are well-behaved, but in reality, we don't know what anybody's life looks like.

Comparing yourself to others it's fruitless and a trap of the enemy. It's a trap that keeps you stuck in a perpetual cycle of comparison. It may be hard not to look at someone else's life and envy it. There will always be somebody who has more or can do more than you if that is your focus.

But the real goal is to focus on who you are and who you've been called to be so you can do the things that God has called you to do. There is a uniqueness in how God created you. When we get caught in comparison what we're saying to God is, "How you made me was not enough"; when in fact you are more than enough.

> *"No, in all these things we are more than conquerors through him who loved us."*
> *Romans 8:37 (NIV)*

Just the thought of saying that to God did not make me "enough" is a very sobering thought to think (I would never want to say that to God). God knew exactly what He was doing when he made you. He knew who and what you would be. He knew all the trials and tribulations you face and even made provisions for those. There is nothing too hard for God.

QUIET TIME

Do you secretly find yourself comparing yourself to others?

PRAYER

God help me to embrace who you created me to be and to remember that I am more than enough. In Jesus' name, Amen.

DAY 07

GIRL, WHO'S "WILL" DO YOU WANT?

Did you know God has a will for your life, it was a package deal when you were born. Many times we base our worth and value on the circumstances of how we entered the world. None of us were accidentally created. Even our parents didn't plan for us. God knew we were to be. He said your life is for a purpose and He decided your birth date.

There is a divine purpose for your life. Every one of us fits into the perfect will of God to do exactly what God has called us to do and to be exactly who He's called us to be.

But we have to choose it. Yes, you must choose to follow God's will. There are two "Wills" our "Will" and what we want to do and then there is God's "Will". God's will is the one that leads us down the path that he has created for us.

> *"Trust in the Lord with all your heart and lean not on your own understanding; in all your ways submit to him, and he will make your paths straight." Proverbs 3:5-6 (NIV)*

God is not intrusive; He will not impose His will on you. You have to choose it. We have free will, and I love that we get to have free will. God didn't make us to be robots but He made us to have choices. And in that choice, we get to choose Him. We get to choose to ask Him to lead and guide us down the path He wants us to go because He is leading and guiding us. He sees all and knows all.

QUIET TIME

Have you chosen to follow God's will for your life? or are you struggling to understand His will for your life?

PRAYER

God, help me to choose your "Will" for my life, because I know that is the best "Will" for me. I only want to be in your Will. In Jesus' name, Amen.

DAY 08

GIRL, I GOT QUESTIONS

Is prayer a part of your everyday life? Do you wake up early enough to make time to spend in prayer with God? Do you seek His guidance and wisdom for your day ahead, asking Him to lead you in all that you do? How important is prayer to you, or are you rushing through the motions, too busy to pause and pray?

> "Rejoice always, pray continually, give thanks in all circumstances; for this is God's will for you in Christ Jesus." 1 Thessalonians 5:16-18 (NIV)

Sometimes, prayer can become something we only turn to in times of crisis or when bad things happen in our lives. But what if prayer became a regular part of your day, a place where you turn first, before you complain or call a friend? What if, when things happen in your life, your first response was, "Let me stop and pray"? When you begin to invite God into every area of your life-whether things are going well or not, you open the door for Him to work through you in ways you could never imagine.

A life of prayer is a life where God can truly use you. He can speak to you, show you things, and guide you with divine wisdom and clarity. You will start to see His hand in the smallest of details and feel His presence in everything you do. Prayer is not just for the hard times; it is the way to stay connected to the One who knows all, sees all, and holds your future in His hands. If prayer is not currently a part of your daily life, this is your moment to make it a priority and experience the power of a life rooted in constant communication with God.

QUIET TIME

Take a few moments to reflect on your prayer life. Are you prioritizing prayer and making time to seek God daily? If not, consider what changes you can make to invite Him into your daily routine.

PRAYER

God, help me to make You and prayer a priority in my life. I want to seek Your guidance, wisdom, and strength in all that I do, and acknowledge the power of who You are in every moment. In Jesus' name, Amen.

DAY 09

GIRL, IT'S TIME TO CHECK IN

Let's talk about self-care as a way to honor your life and the temple that God has given you. When you think about self-care, it's not just about the outer parts like taking care of your hair, nails, and makeup or having a spa day with your girlfriends or any of those things. That's part of it, and that's part of taking care of your temple. But there's also self-care in regards to taking care of your spiritual life, and emotional health and checking in with yourself. What practices do you have in place for that?

> *"Do you not know that your bodies are temples of the Holy Spirit, who is in you, whom you have received from God? You are not your own; you were bought at a price. Therefore honor God with your bodies."*
> 1 Corinthians 6:19-20 (NIV)

How do you check in with yourself? Do you know when you are having an off day or when something is eating at you emotionally? How do you tend to do that? Where do you store your thoughts? Or are they always just swirling around in your head? Do you take time to meditate, sit still, and be quiet? Do you take time to journal? These are practices that you can incorporate into your daily life to help with your self-care. Even reading these daily devotionals; is part of your self-care.

There are also times when you may need to speak to a professional for your mental health care and this is a part of taking care of yourself. You may need therapy and Jesus, and that's ok because he gave us a Therapist for a reason. Use the tool that God has given you.

QUIET GIRL SZN

QUIET TIME

Take a moment to check in with yourself,
How are you doing?

PRAYER

God help me to honor my temple and to continue to make sure that I am checking in and taking care of not just my physical but also my mental, emotional, and spiritual state. In Jesus' name, Amen.

DAY 10

GIRL, IT'S NOT WHAT YOU THINK

I used to think purpose was a thing that we were always searching for. Everywhere you turned everyone had the same questions. "What is my purpose in life?" I have since come to think of purpose in a different way. I realize there is purpose in everything we do.

Since my discovery, it took away the all-elusive purpose search. It took away the longing for something that was outside myself and allowed me to see purpose all around me. I believe when we view purpose like this it stops us from running around in a rat race trying to chase something that we ultimately can't see. When we view it from those lenses we can start being present to experience the moments we are living in.

If you look around you there is purpose in everything you do. Similar to always focusing on the destination and not enjoying the journey. It's all about the journey; purpose can be seized on the journey. When you look at life as a journey, you get an opportunity to discover purpose in those moments.

> *"And we know that in all things God works for the good of those who love him, who have been called according to his purpose."*
> *Romans 8:28 (NIV)*

Purpose is not a thing that you chase; it's not a thing that you find. But I believe that purpose "Is". It IS present all around us. There is a purpose in this book that you are reading. There's purpose in that chair that you are sitting in. There's a purpose in everything. Just stop and take a look around. You will see purpose in absolutely everything. If you stop and look at your life, you will see there is a purpose in everywhere you go and everything you do.

QUIET TIME

Take a moment to reflect on the purpose of the stage of life you are in now and retrace the steps you took to get there. Do you see the purpose in the journey?

PRAYER

Lord help me to see purpose in all I do and to show up as my best self in every place you take me on this journey. In Jesus' name, Amen.

DAY 11

GIRL, I SEE YOU

I think it's Kendrick Lamar who has the song that says, "Be humble, stay down." Everyone is striving for success. Everyone wants to make something of their life. There is a sense of satisfaction that we've attached our worth and value to in correlation to the things that we do.

For so long as I can remember all I ever wanted to do was make my family and friends proud of me. Because of the difficulties and the various traumas I've experienced many areas of my life were a mess.

I was always striving to do something great in my life so that I could finally feel seen and validated. One day God helped me to realize that my worth and value had nothing to do with the things I achieved or didn't achieve. My worth and value were because of who God says I am and who He created me to be. The fact that I was born meant that my life was worth something.

> "For we are God's handiwork, created in Christ Jesus to do good works, which God prepared in advance for us to do."
> Ephesians 2:10 (NIV)

When I understood this, it gave a new meaning to the hustle and the striving. It gave a new meaning to me trying to prove to myself and others that my life is valuable and I am worthy. Not that it didn't matter, but for the first time I saw myself the way God intended me to see me. And that was all that mattered. So whatever it is you're striving for, think about the reason why you're striving for it. Think about what you want and why you want it.

QUIET TIME

What are you striving for? When attaining it, what would it mean to you?

PRAYER

God help me to be and do all you have called me to for your Glory. In Jesus' name, Amen.

DAY 12

GIRL, DON'T BE SCARED

I hate that we allow fear to rob and stop us from doing so many things in our lives. We give fear too much credit. Many aspects of what we fear are virtually non-existent, it is a bunch of "What ifs" that we have conjured up in our minds. The biggest one that holds us back is the fear of the unknown. Fear has been the number one killer of our passion and dreams. We fear what we don't know and we fear what we can't control.

What if you practiced saying to yourself "I don't know how this is going to turn out, and yes, I am concerned about the unknown, but I am going to do it anyway"?," or when you feel fear start with these 2 questions:

1. Am I in danger, or is someone I love in danger? (usually, the answer is no)
2. What exactly am I afraid of? (Tell the truth it will help you get to the root of it and then it will help you dispel the myth of it.)

> "For the Spirit God gave us does not make us timid, but gives us power, love and self-discipline." 2 Timothy 1:7 (NIV)

Another thing we fear is what we call failure, but I like to call them lessons. "Yep, that didn't work, okay -next." Just because something you tried may have failed that doesn't mean that you are a failure. It may mean that you need to try something else. Give yourself permission to try things without allowing the fear of failure or the unknown to rule your life. Sometimes you have to feel the fear and do it anyway while you are being reminded that God gave you Power.

QUIET TIME

Have you been allowing fear to rule your life? How can you change that and stand in the power that God has given you?

PRAYER

God help me to trust to stand in the power you have given me and not allow fear to rule my life. In Jesus' name, Amen.

DAY 13

GIRL, YOU BETTER THANK GOD

I am thankful for what God has done in my life. When I look back over my life and think of all the things that God has brought me through, I have no other choice but to be thankful. I think about all the things I've been saved from that could have been worse—times when I didn't know how things were going to turn out, yet God's hand was there all along. He was guiding me, protecting me, and providing for me, even in moments when I couldn't see it. The more I reflect on His goodness, the more I see the impact of having God in my life and the difference it makes. I am thankful for His daily grace and mercy. I shudder to think where my life would be without Him.

"Give thanks to the Lord, for he is good; his love endures forever." Psalm 107:1 (NIV)

When you look back on your life, do you see God's hand at work? Can you see all the times He saved you, both from things you were aware of and dangers you didn't even know existed? The fact that we wake up each day, with breath in our lungs and the ability to think clearly, is a blessing in itself. We may not always recognize how blessed we are, but when we take a moment to reflect, we realize just how much we have to be thankful for. The truth is, we could spend every waking hour giving thanks, and it still wouldn't be enough to fully express our gratitude.

Being thankful shifts our mindset and draws us closer to God. It changes our perspective, reminding us of His faithfulness and provision. Gratitude helps us focus not on what we lack, but on what we've already been given. It allows us to recognize the ways in which God continuously shows up for us.

QUIET TIME

When was the last time you sat and truly gave thanks to God for all He has done? Take some time now and name a few things you're thankful for. Let your heart overflow with gratitude.

PRAYER

God, I am thankful for who You are and how You continually keep me. Thank You for Your love, guidance, and protection from dangers seen and unseen. I trust You and give You all the glory for the work You are doing in my life. In Jesus' name, Amen.

DAY **14**

GIRL, CHECK YOUR CIRCLE

How are your relationships? Do you have good relationships with people? Do you have good friendships? Do you know how to be a good friend? Are you caring, loving, and supportive? How do you handle conflicts with your friends? When you don't agree, what do you do? Are you able to communicate your thoughts and feelings in a way that doesn't necessarily end the relationship?

"As iron sharpens iron, so one person sharpens another." Proverbs 27:17 (NIV)

Being a friend is a great responsibility. Friendship is a meaningful relationship that requires intentionality. When you choose to be someone's friend, it involves vulnerability, love, care, and trustworthiness. Healthy friendships help both people grow and provide support in ways that foster spiritual and emotional well-being. A good friendship is not just about having fun together but being there during tough times, offering encouragement, and holding each other accountable. When God is at the center of your relationships, He can guide you in building deep connections that glorify Him.

At times, friendships face challenges, conflicts, misunderstandings, or differing opinions. How we navigate those moments speaks volumes about the strength of our relationships. Are we quick to forgive and resolve issues, or do we let conflicts fester? Are we transparent and honest, or do we shy away from necessary conversations? Learning to communicate effectively and lovingly, even in disagreement, helps preserve friendships and allows both people to grow.

We also must be careful not to gossip or share things inappropriately about our friends behind their backs. Loyalty and trust are key elements of friendship, and breaking those bonds can do lasting harm. Our friendships reflect our character, and how we treat others shows the kind of people we are becoming.

QUIET TIME

Take a few moments to assess your friendships. Who is in your circle? Do they exhibit qualities of a good friend? More importantly, assess yourself—are you being the kind of friend God has called you to be?

PRAYER

God, help me to be a loving, caring, and supportive friend. Teach me how to nurture the relationships You have placed in my life, and help me to reflect Your love in all my friendships. Show me how to handle conflicts with grace and to always be trustworthy. In Jesus' name, Amen.

DAY 15

GIRL, REST YOUR SOUL

Are you resting? Rest is important. I do not play about my naps; my whole family knows it. Especially on Sundays, that after-church, after-dinner nap hits differently. My soul and my body are fed, and I'm good, lol. You can't keep going, going, and going—don't let that Energizer Bunny fool you. Rest is for rejuvenation. You need to take time to relax. I love that God built sleep into our lives. I think that's just so dope that He said, "Okay, at nighttime, go to sleep," because it's how our bodies heal; it's how our cells rejuvenate. It's also how He speaks to some of us. Therefore, I say rest is spiritual.

> *"Come to me, all you who are weary and burdened, and I will give you rest."*
> *Matthew 11:28 (NIV)*

Rest is not just about sleep; it's about peace for the mind and spirit. When you're constantly on the move, it's easy to get caught up in the hustle and forget how essential it is to pause. Rest allows you to recalibrate and reflect on the direction you're headed. It's in these moments that you gain clarity about the next steps in your life. Without taking time to rest, it's easy to make hasty decisions, act out of frustration, and lose sight of God's leading. Rest doesn't just heal the body; it renews the spirit. God wants us to come to Him when we are weary, and in Him, we will find the rest that strengthens us for the journey ahead.

When we take time to rest, we are allowing God to restore us, preparing us to walk into our purpose with fresh energy and perspective. So whether it's a nap or a quiet moment spent in His presence, don't neglect to take the rest your body and soul need.

QUIET GIRL SZN

QUIET TIME

When was the last time you had good rest and you felt really rejuvenated? Do you need to incorporate more periods of rest in your life?

PRAYER

God help me to get the proper rest I need and to not over-exert myself. I want to be available and ready to do the things you have for me. In Jesus' name, Amen.

DAY 16

GIRL, DO YOU RECOGNIZE HIS VOICE?

Have you ever heard people say, "God told me," or "God spoke to me"? I say it too. But then I hear others ask, "How do you know when God is speaking?" It's the same way you know when your mom, dad, son, daughter, or sister is speaking—you know their voice. You've spent time with them, listened to their voice, and you recognize how they sound. Even if they call you on the telephone and you don't see their face, you know it's them. You know their voice, and that's how you get to know God's voice as well.

It's about building a relationship and spending intimate time with God, cultivating that connection so that when He speaks, you can discern whether it's your voice or His.

> "My sheep hear my voice, and I know them, and they follow me." (John 10:27, NIV)

I typically know when I am speaking and when God is speaking to me. He often uses my voice because I pray out loud, and when I talk to Him, I'm always speaking out loud. I can tell the difference between what I say and when it's Him speaking through me because I've spent enough time with Him and developed that relationship enough to know His voice.

The only way you'll get to know God's voice is by spending time with Him. It's not always an audible voice; sometimes, God speaks in silence. He can speak in a still, small whisper, or through others. God is speaking through everything around you. How He chooses to speak to you depends on the relationship you have with Him. He'll speak to you in a way that you will hear Him, and when He does, it will be so evident and clear that it could only be Him.

QUIET GIRL SZN

QUIET TIME

How can you cultivate more intentional time with God this week to better recognize His voice in your life?

PRAYER

Lord, help me to spend more time with You so that I may know Your voice clearly and follow Your guidance. In Jesus' name, Amen.

DAY 17

GIRL, YOU BETTER CELEBRATE

When was the last time you celebrated the wins in your life? Are you the type to celebrate? I know that sometimes I don't always celebrate myself. I move from one thing to the next, appreciating the victory but not really celebrating it or making a big deal of it. But I believe it's important that we recognize and celebrate our wins.

A celebration doesn't always have to mean a big fancy party or a large cake. Sometimes, celebrating your victories means simply acknowledging them and taking a moment to truly appreciate them, rather than just moving on to the next task and glossing over it. When we start celebrating our wins, life gains more meaning. It becomes more purposeful. Celebrating gives us a chance to look forward to our achievements and find joy in the journey, not just the destination. When you celebrate, you're looking forward to it because you know it's coming.

> "The Lord has done great things for us,
> and we are filled with joy."
> (Psalm 126:3, NIV)

However, when you never really celebrate and just move from one thing to the next, life can lose its excitement. It's important to celebrate because life can be hard, and every achievement deserves recognition. If you accomplish something, acknowledge it. For example, writing this devotional is me doing something significant. If you knew the journey it took for me to get here, you'd understand why I plan to celebrate when this is done. Are you celebrating? Celebrate the journey. Celebrate your wins. Celebrate your victories.

QUIET TIME

What small or big win in your life can you take the time to celebrate today?

PRAYER

Lord, help me to pause and celebrate the victories You've given me, finding joy in the journey as much as in the destination. In Jesus' name, Amen.

DAY 18

GIRL, I DON'T DOUBT IT

Doubt has this funny way of creeping in. Especially when you decide to do something, doubt finds a way to sneak in. Suddenly, all these reasons appear, telling you why you can't do it or making you feel inadequate. But if you strengthen your faith, even in the face of adversity and uncertainty, and push past the doubt and fear, you'll be amazed at the results you'll see. It's almost as if you can become unstoppable once you make up your mind to be that way. Doubt may come because you don't know how things will turn out, but it just can't stay.

When you don't believe something is possible, it can start to take a toll on you, hindering you from doing what you truly want to do. In those moments, it's important to ask God to help your unbelief and to affirm that you're doing the right thing in the right way. When doubt becomes too loud, pause and remind yourself of who you are in Christ. Ask God to not only silence the doubt but also to give you the courage to press forward, even when the path seems uncertain. Remember that God's plans for you are good and filled with hope, and when you walk by faith, you step into alignment with His purpose for your life.

> "Immediately the boy's father exclaimed, 'I do believe; help me overcome my unbelief!'"
> (Mark 9:24, NIV)

Belief is a powerful thing. You will be amazed at what you can achieve when you stop doubting yourself and remove those limiting thoughts. Trusting in God's timing and His ability to guide you will unlock doors you didn't even realize were possible. Don't allow doubt to hold you back from the destiny God has prepared for you.

QUIET GIRL SZN

QUIET TIME

What is one area in your life where you need to push past doubt and trust in God's ability to guide you?

PRAYER

God, I ask that You help me overcome my unbelief and strengthen my faith. When doubt tries to enter my mind, remind me that with You, all things are possible. Help me to trust Your plan and to move forward with confidence, knowing You are leading me. In Jesus' name, Amen.

DAY 19

GIRL, HE IS YOUR STRENGTH

There are times when you won't always feel strong. Not everything you do will be your greatest strength. There may be areas where you feel weak and even defeated. But during those times, we can ask God to give us the strength to move forward, to do the things He's called us to do.

There are many times when I think about what I'm doing, and I don't always feel confident. I don't always feel courageous. I don't always feel strong. In those moments, I have to pray and ask God to lead me, guide me, and give me the strength and courage to do what He's called me to do. Even in my weakness, God says that He is strong.

Sometimes, I don't know what to do. In those moments of weakness, it feels vulnerable because we want to always put our best foot forward, but that may not always be the case.

> "But he said to me, 'My grace is sufficient for you, for my power is made perfect in weakness.' Therefore I will boast all the more gladly about my weaknesses, so that Christ's power may rest on me." (2 Corinthians 12:9, NIV)

In those times, that's when you can draw on God's strength to lead and guide you. I love how even with faith, you can have faith as small as a mustard seed. Have you seen the size of a mustard seed? Think about God's strength in you, helping you to do things you didn't think you could do. When we get to the other side, the victory that comes as a result—that's what I like to call amazing grace, how sweet the sound that saved a wretch like me- I once was lost, but now I'm found; I was blind, but now I see.

QUIET TIME

Where in your life do you need to lean on God's strength instead of your own?

PRAYER

Lord, in my weakness, I ask for your strength to carry me through and accomplish what you've called me to do. In Jesus' name, Amen.

DAY 20

GIRL, DON'T BE BITTER

Are You a Forgiving Person? It's not always easy to forgive others when you feel that they have wronged you. Forgiveness is challenging because it often comes with offense, and being offended is painful. It's hurtful when someone wrongs you, misleads you, or misjudges you.

We've always heard and been taught that forgiveness is not for the other person; it's for you. The interesting thing about unforgiveness is that it creates a root of bitterness that can take hold in your life, not the other person's. When bitterness takes root, it begins to infect other areas of your life, turning you bitter. Just a little bit of bitterness can change the flavor of your life, like a drop of something bitter in your water. You don't want bitterness to consume you, which is why forgiveness is so important.

Forgiveness is freeing. It frees you to live the life you were called to live without holding onto the offense of whatever was said or done to you.

> *"Be kind and compassionate to one another, forgiving each other, just as in Christ God forgave you."*
> *(Ephesians 4:32, NIV)*

Even if the person never apologizes or admits they were wrong, it's important for your well-being that you can forgive so you can live a healthy, grateful life—a life that God honors. When you hold unforgiveness in your heart, how can you go to God and ask Him to forgive you if you haven't forgiven others?

QUIET TIME

Is there someone in your life you need to forgive, even if they haven't apologized? How can you start the process of forgiveness today?

PRAYER

Lord, help me to forgive others as You have forgiven me, freeing my heart from bitterness and filling it with Your love. In Jesus' name, Amen.

DAY **21**

GIRL, WATCH YOUR MOUTH

How are you using your words? The words that come out of your mouth—are they words that build up or words that tear down? Words guide your life. If you ever want to understand where your life is headed, think about the words you speak. Are you saying things like "I can't" or "I will never"? Every word you speak is the equivalent of speaking life or speaking death.

Are your words encouraging and inspiring? Do you use them to uplift others or even yourself? I know that life can be hard, and there are so many outside forces at play, but the words we speak, how we live, and how we think are choices. We get to choose how we respond, even in moments that are not the greatest.

Your words are charting the course of your life, so it's important to pay attention to what you say. Sometimes, it may mean saying nothing at all because words can also cause damage.

> *"Likewise, the tongue is a small part of the body, but it makes great boasts. Consider what a great forest is set on fire by a small spark. The tongue also is a fire, a world of evil among the parts of the body. It corrupts the whole body, sets the whole course of one's life on fire, and is itself set on fire by hell."*
> *(James 3:5-6, NIV)*

There's an old adage that says, "Sticks and stones can break my bones, but words will never hurt." That's not true, and I don't know who said it, but it's not true. Words can do a lot of damage, but words can also do a lot of good. The choice is yours. Your words can move you forward, or they can move you backward. How are you using your words? If you were to record yourself for one full day and played back everything you said, would you be surprised by how you sounded? Would you be surprised by the things you said? Try it.

QUIET GIRL SZN

QUIET TIME

What kind of impact are your words having on your life and the lives of others? How can you be more intentional with your words?

PRAYER

Lord, help me to use my words wisely, to speak life and not death, and to uplift others and myself with the power of my tongue. In Jesus' name, Amen.

DAY 22

GIRL, BE PATIENT

No one wants to hear the word "wait." Waiting seems long. Waiting seems pointless. But waiting can be necessary. You might be waiting for something that's not ready yet. Imagine you were cooking chicken, and it needed 20 minutes in the air fryer, but you decided you didn't want to wait the full 20 minutes. If you took it out after just five minutes and ate it, you'd get sick. Would you wait? Then waiting is necessary.

Waiting helps things to develop. The thing you need in your life during the waiting period might be exactly what will help you in the season you're entering. It may not be because what you're waiting for isn't ready; sometimes it's because *you* aren't ready. So many things are cultivated during the waiting season—character, resilience, and endurance—all of which are essential for different parts of your life.

Don't begrudge or bemoan the waiting process. Don't always be so impatient and think that you need things right now. Waiting helps build your endurance. Waiting helps build your resilience. Waiting allows you to trust in God's timing because He knows all and sees all.

> "But those who hope in the Lord will renew their strength. They will soar on wings like eagles; they will run and not grow weary, they will walk and not be faint." (Isaiah 40:31, NIV)

Our sight is very limited. We only see what's in front of us, beside us, around us, and behind us. But God sees the bigger picture, and during the waiting period, we may not understand its purpose. However, if we trust in God's timing, we'll find that it's always perfect.

QUIET TIME

In what area of your life are you struggling to wait, and how can you trust God's timing more fully?

PRAYER

Lord, help me to embrace the waiting season, trusting that Your timing is perfect and that You are preparing me for what lies ahead. In Jesus' name, Amen.

DAY 23

GIRL, RELAX YOU ARE ON A JOURNEY

I want you to celebrate your life and how far you've come. If you stopped for a moment and looked back at your life, you'd see that you have come a very long way. Sometimes, while we are in the midst of things, we don't always pay attention to how far we've come. We tend to focus on how far we still have to go. But today, I want you to pause and reflect on your journey.

Take a look back at all the things you've been through, the places you've been, and the people who have come and gone in your life. Everything you've experienced matters—it's all part of a bigger picture. We often focus on where we're going and think about the destination, but we don't always pay attention to the journey that has been shaping and cultivating us along the way.

Realize that you've come this far by faith, with God leading, guiding, and directing you, as He promised never to leave nor forsake you.

> *"Being confident of this, that he who began a good work in you will carry it on to completion until the day of Christ Jesus." (Philippians 1:6, NIV)*

So, I want you to reflect on the journey. Appreciate the journey. Understand and honor the journey you've been on, knowing that it's all a part of your life story and a piece of the bigger picture. As you reflect, think about all the times God has had His hand on your life—where you can visibly see His presence and know that He's always working and willing in your life. Trust that all things work together for good.

QUIET TIME

How has God guided and shaped you through your life journey, and how can you celebrate the progress you've made?

PRAYER

Lord, I thank You for the journey You've brought me through. Help me to appreciate how far I've come and to trust that You will continue the good work You've started in me. In Jesus' name, Amen.

DAY 24

GIRL, ITS OK TO CHANGE YOUR MIND

Renewing your mind first starts with transforming your thoughts. When you think about transforming your thoughts, it begins with giving yourself new information. This can come in many different forms, but the one I want to focus on is renewing your mind through God's Word. There are so many biblical principles in God's Word that we sometimes overlook, either because of the stories or the age of the Bible, without fully understanding how they apply to our lives. However, there are numerous ways to read, apply, and understand these timeless truths. I believe these stories are designed with purpose.

"Do not conform to the pattern of this world, but be transformed by the renewing of your mind. Then you will be able to test and approve what God's will is—his good, pleasing, and perfect will." (Romans 12:2, NIV)

God's Word is so powerful. It contains many principles that can lead and guide your life, helping you transform and change it. Without tools, it can be difficult for individuals to change their lives. But God's Word provides those tools to help you on this journey because, otherwise, you only know what you know. When you discover new information, it gives you a new path to take, guiding you down a different journey.

If you want to live a different life, you have to start by thinking differently. And if you want something different, you're going to have to do something different.

QUIET TIME

What steps can you take today to renew your mind through God's Word and transform your thoughts?

PRAYER

Lord, help me to renew my mind by immersing myself in Your Word, so that I may transform my thoughts and live according to your will. In Jesus' name, Amen.

DAY 25

GIRL, I'M PRAYING FOR YOU

Do you pray for others, or are your prayers centered around yourself?

Are your prayers focused on what you need, what you want, and what you want God to do for you? That may not be your story, but it certainly was mine. When I examined my prayer life, I realized it was so self-centered. I understand—you have to pray for yourself because if you don't, there's no guarantee that others are praying for you. But if your prayers are only about yourself and not for anyone else, that's where the issue lies.

There is power in praying for others. There is power in coming together, touching and agreeing, and asking God to move in someone else's life. Whether it's praying for a loved one, a coworker, a friend, or someone who is sick, our prayers can make a difference. Often, we tell people, "Oh, I'll pray for you," or "I'm going to pray for you," and it sounds good. We may even have good intentions, but sometimes we don't follow through.

What if we made a conscious decision to start praying for others more intentionally?

> "Therefore confess your sins to each other and pray for each other so that you may be healed. The prayer of a righteous person is powerful and effective." (James 5:16, NIV)

When I started praying for others, it changed my outlook. I began to develop more of a heart for people, genuinely wanting God to work in their lives. It helped me to shift the focus off of myself and prevented everything from being self-centered. Today, consider making a conscious effort to pray for someone else besides yourself.

QUIET TIME

Who in your life could benefit from your prayers today, and how can you make praying for others a regular part of your prayer life?

PRAYER

Lord, help me to focus not only on my own needs but also on the needs of others, praying for them with a sincere heart. In Jesus' name, Amen.

DAY 26

GIRL, LISTEN

God is speaking all around you. You may not realize it, but God is speaking in all the things that you are doing. God can give you strategy, and sometimes you have to learn how to control your emotions so that you can think clearly enough to hear what He is saying and see what He is trying to show you. Often, our emotions can fog our ability to see the big picture. When those moments come, we need to take a moment to stop, pray, and ask God, "What is it that You are trying to say to me?" I always ask, "What do You want me to see? What do You want me to hear? What do You want me to know?" You would be amazed that when you ask those questions, you will get answers.

Too often, we don't stop to ask the right questions. Instead, we act based on our emotions and feelings, which is not the best way to make decisions.

> *"Be still, and know that I am God; I will be exalted among the nations, I will be exalted in the earth." (Psalm 46:10, NIV)*

When you live a life that is dialed in and leaned into God, He will show you the steps He wants you to take. He'll reveal the things He needs you to see and let you hear what you need to hear, but you have to ask. God will not override your will or force His will upon you. There are times when I believe the Holy Spirit, in His infinite wisdom, will intercede on your behalf, but you have to invite Him into your life. Allow God to be Lord over your life so that you can know the direction He has for you, the things He wants you to do, and how He wants you to do them.

QUIET TIME

How can you better control your emotions to hear God's voice and see the direction He is leading you?

PRAYER

Lord, help me to quiet my emotions and lean into Your wisdom so that I may hear Your voice and follow Your guidance. In Jesus' name, Amen.

DAY 27

GIRL, YOU BETTER ASK

How do you make decisions?

What do you use as a measuring tool or blueprint when making decisions? Are you just out here guessing or relying solely on your own knowledge? Do you pray for wisdom? God tells us that we can ask Him for wisdom, and He will give it to us liberally. I try not to make decisions on my own without seeking wisdom and guidance from God because I know that I've made some terrible choices in my life. There were many times when I did not consult God, did not ask, and didn't even think to ask. If I'm being honest, many times I didn't pray at all. I just made the decision I thought was best at the moment. Sometimes it worked out, and sometimes it didn't.

> *"If any of you lacks wisdom, you should ask God, who gives generously to all without finding fault, and it will be given to you." (James 1:5, NIV)*

But if you can get into the habit of stopping to pray before making decisions—and not only stopping to pray but also listening—I believe it will make a significant difference. Give God an opportunity to respond, and He will speak to you in the way that He knows you will hear Him. When He responds, it's clear, concise, and without a doubt. There is a peace that surrounds His guidance.

I don't know how you've been processing decisions in the past, but I encourage you to include God in your decision-making process going forward.

QUIET TIME

How can you make a habit of seeking God's wisdom before making decisions in your life?

PRAYER

Lord, help me to seek Your wisdom and guidance before making decisions, trusting that You will lead me clearly and with peace. In Jesus' name, Amen.

DAY 28

GIRL, PAY ATTENTION

Do you know when to let go?

Do you know when to walk away? Do you know when to say "uncle," when enough is enough? Do you know when time is up? Do you know when it's time to close a door? Even when it's time to close doors, we should always close them gently. Do you know when one season has ended? There are signs to it all. If you pay attention, it's like knowing when you've overstayed your welcome at someone's place—you just know when it's time to go.

Are you paying attention to the cues around you? Seasons change. It doesn't always rain, and it's not always winter. Just as the sun doesn't always shine, each season comes with its own level of preparation. In the summer, you wear fewer clothes; in the winter, you wear more.

> "There is a time for everything, and a season for every activity under the heavens."
> (Ecclesiastes 3:1, NIV)

We determine the season by how it feels, and it's the same process when discerning the seasons of your life. When seasons are changing, there is a shift in the atmosphere. There is a change that gives you an indication that something is shifting, something is changing. Are you paying attention to the shifts? Are you noticing the changes that are leading you in different directions?

Knowing when to move, when to go, and when to stay is a matter of being in tune with God. It's about paying attention and trusting the leading of the Holy Spirit, who will guide you. Pay attention to what's going on in your life. Pay attention to the shifts and the changes.

QUIET GIRL SZN

QUIET TIME

Are there areas in your life where you sense a shift in seasons? How can you trust God's guidance in discerning when to let go or move forward?

PRAYER

Lord, help me to recognize the changing seasons in my life and trust Your guidance to know when it's time to let go or move forward. In Jesus' name, Amen.

DAY 29

GIRL, JUST SAY YES

Have you said yes to God?

I mean a literal "Yes," where you open your mouth and say, "Yes, God, I will do what You have called me to do." "Yes, God, I will say what You tell me to say." "Yes, God, I will go where You tell me to go." Saying yes to God changes your life. It changes everything about you. It changes the lens through which you start to see life. When you open yourself to His direction, you surrender control, and in that surrender, you find the peace and fulfillment you've been searching for. There is a freedom that comes with saying "Yes", knowing that God will equip you for what He has called you to do.

Saying yes to God means you are available and that He can use you. When you say yes to God, your life will never be the same. He will use you in ways you didn't even think were possible. He will have you do things you didn't think you could do. He will stretch you, grow you, and walk with you through every challenge and blessing along the way. Often, we fear saying yes because we don't know what it will require of us. But trust that God's plans for your life are far greater than your own, and when you say yes, you are stepping into a divine purpose that will bless not only you but also others around you.

> "Then I heard the voice of the Lord saying, 'Whom shall I send? And who will go for us?' And I said, 'Here am I. Send me!'"
> (Isaiah 6:8, NIV)

Your "Yes" is one of the most important things you can say to God. He is looking for available souls. The harvest is ripe, but the laborers are few. God has a need for you. This world needs you. Someone needs you. They need what you have to offer. They need who you are. Your presence in someone's life is essential. When you say yes, you become a vessel for God's will on earth, touching lives in ways you may never fully comprehend. Are you ready to say yes? Are you willing to say yes? Have you said yes?

QUIET TIME

What is holding you back from saying a full, wholehearted yes to God, and how can you take a step toward that yes today?

PRAYER

Lord, I say yes to You. Use me as you will, and guide me in the path you have set before me. In Jesus' name, Amen.

DAY 30

GIRL, YOU ARE NOT IN CONTROL

Struggling with control. We think we're in control, but we are not. We have such a false sense of control, believing that if we can control things, we can control the outcome and even control other people. We think we can control what they say and do so that we can be comfortable. But that's not true. We have a distorted understanding of what control is and what it means.

When we think we're in control, what we're really saying is that we don't trust God to lead us in the right direction. We don't trust that He'll make the right decisions and choices for us, and we don't trust that He'll send the right people into our lives. So, we try to manipulate and orchestrate things to maintain control.

> "Many are the plans in a person's heart, but it is the Lord's purpose that prevails." (Proverbs 19:21, NIV)

A lot of control issues stem from past trauma, where people in our lives didn't treat us as they should have, manipulated us, or did things they shouldn't have done. As a coping mechanism, we try to control situations, but it's a false sense of security—we are not in control as much as we think we are. It's nice to think we are, but we're not.

One of the best things we can do is trust God to lead us and maneuver in our lives. This means taking our hands off situations and allowing God to move people—and even us—out of places where we don't belong. When you trust Him, trust that He will work things together for good, even when, on the surface and in the moment, they don't seem that way. Know that it's all working out for your good.

It's like Mr. Miyagi in "The Karate Kid," making him wax on and wax off, and he couldn't understand why. Sometimes we don't understand why things happen, and there may be a time when you will understand—or maybe you won't. But know that it's all working together for your good and God will show you when to wax on and was off.

QUIET GIRL SZN

QUIET TIME

What areas of your life are you trying to control, and how can you begin to trust God to lead and guide you instead?

PRAYER

Lord, help me to release my need for control and trust in your perfect plan for my life, knowing that You work all things together for my good. In Jesus' name, Amen.

DAY 31

GIRL, YOU ARE CONSISTENT

You are more consistent than you think, for years, you may have told yourself that you're not consistent, and over time, you've allowed that belief to settle deep in your subconscious. But here's the truth: you are consistent. I see it in how you show up every morning. You take time to talk to God, to pray, and to reflect. You've committed to these devotionals, pouring out your heart day after day. This is consistency.

Now, I want you to take that same energy and apply it to other areas of your life. Think about how you consistently show up for work, for your children, or for your friends. Transfer that same dedication to the things you want for yourself. If your "why" is strong enough, it will fuel the consistency you need to accomplish your goals.

And here's a little reminder: even in saying you're not consistent, you are being consistent—consistent with your words. Imagine if you changed those words to align with the direction you want to go. If you consistently speak life over your dreams and goals, your actions will start to follow. So, let's flip the script. You are consistent. The proof is in your actions, your prayers, and your daily efforts. Don't let a limiting belief hold you back any longer.

> *"Let us not become weary in doing good, for at the proper time we will reap a harvest if we do not give up." Galatians 6:9 (NIV)*

Remember, changing your perspective changes your life. Stop focusing on what didn't happen in the past and start acknowledging what you are doing now. Take pride in knowing that you are doing your best and that you're continually growing. Celebrate your consistency in all areas of life, and keep trusting the process.

QUIET GIRL SZN

QUIET TIME

Where in your life have you shown consistency, and how can you transfer that same effort to your personal goals?

PRAYER

Lord, thank You for revealing the areas where I have shown consistency. Help me to align my actions with the goals and dreams You've placed in my heart. Strengthen my resolve to stay the course and remind me daily that I am capable of following through. In Jesus' name, Amen.

DAY 32

GIRL, TAKE SOMETHING OFF YOUR PLATE

Have you ever found yourself feeling overwhelmed?

Being overwhelmed is when you have all these things going on at once. I was thinking about being overwhelmed the other day, and I realized that overwhelm is when what you think you are controlling has now turned into chaos. It's you trying to control everything and do it all at once. Sometimes, when we have too many things to do, we look at everything at once, and that can be overwhelming. It can make you feel out of control.

> *"Come to me, all you who are weary and burdened, and I will give you rest."*
> (Matthew 11:28, NIV)

Overcoming overwhelm is about how you compartmentalize the things you need to do and determine what's important and what's not. It's about how you view things and what systems you have in place to help you manage them. Sometimes, you have to ask yourself if you're putting too much on your plate. Overwhelm can be a real issue when you've taken on too much and given yourself more than you can handle.

When you feel overwhelmed, that's the time to stop and reassess. It helps to start your day with a reassessment, or perhaps end your night with one, to check in with yourself. It's good to ask yourself how you're feeling, what's going on, and what needs to change. What's working and what's not? When you take the time to do this, you can get yourself back on track and reduce those feelings of overwhelm.

QUIET TIME

What steps can you take to reassess and prioritize when you start to feel overwhelmed, and how can you rely on God's strength to find rest?

PRAYER

Lord, when I feel overwhelmed, help me to pause, reassess, and find rest in you, trusting that you will guide me through the chaos. In Jesus' name, Amen.

DAY 33

GIRL, WHAT IS YOUR LIFE FOR?

Answering the call for God to use you can be a scary thing. You don't know where it's going to lead or how it will transform your life. Yet, this is the very essence of faith—trusting that God's plans for you are good, even when the road ahead seems uncertain. When you begin to reflect on your gifts, talents, and abilities, you might find yourself asking, "What is my life even for?" This question pulls you away from the mundane and invites you to seek the purpose God has uniquely placed within you.

In the hustle of daily life, it's easy to become consumed by all the things you feel obligated to do or want to do. But when was the last time you truly stopped to consider the deeper things of life—the things that carry lasting meaning and eternal significance? Often, we operate on autopilot, moving through our routines, but God calls us to something more: a life that serves His Kingdom and aligns with the things that matter most.

> "For I know the plans I have for you," declares the Lord, "plans to prosper you and not to harm you, plans to give you hope and a future."* - Jeremiah 29:11 (NIV)

God's plans are designed to prosper you and give you hope and a future, not just for your own benefit but to make a difference in the world. By answering God's call, you step into a life of purpose, deeply aligned with His will. This means using your gifts to contribute to something greater than yourself. It means seeking the deeper meaning behind everything you do and asking, "How can I use what God has given me to glorify Him and serve others?"

This reflection pulls you beyond the surface, challenging you to consider how your life can make a difference. How can you contribute to things that matter—not just for today, but for eternity? Answering God's call means stepping out in faith and trusting that He is guiding you toward a life that is not only fulfilling but also purposeful in His Kingdom.

QUIET GIRL SZN

QUIET TIME

What gifts, talents, or experiences can you use to serve God's Kingdom, and how can you take the first step in answering His call?

PRAYER

Lord, help me to see beyond the daily routine and understand how I can use the gifts you've given me to make a meaningful impact in this world. In Jesus' name, Amen.

DAY 34

GIRL, STOP WASTING TIME

Do you ever find yourself wasting time?

Just think about it. When you look at your life—the scope of it—and the number of days you have, as if you actually know that number, do you ever think about life in that regard? Do you ever consider what it all means and why we waste time? We waste time talking ourselves in and out of things. We waste time feeling like we're not good enough. We waste time competing and comparing. We waste time on social media. We waste time watching television. We waste so much time.

"Be very careful, then, how you live—not as unwise but as wise, making the most of every opportunity, because the days are evil." (Ephesians 5:15-16, NIV)

Yet, when it comes to meaningful things or things we really want to do, we often tell ourselves that we don't have time. Sometimes, it's not a matter of not having time; it's a matter of not making time. We make time for the things we want to do. We make time for the places we want to go. We make time for the shows we want to watch. We make time for what we think matters to us, but then we make excuses for the other things.

So, how long are you going to keep wasting time as if you have all the time in the world?

QUIET GIRL SZN

QUIET TIME

What areas of your life are you wasting time in, and how can you start making more intentional use of your time?

PRAYER

Lord, help me to be mindful of how I use my time, making the most of every opportunity to live wisely and purposefully. In Jesus' name, Amen.

DAY 35

GIRL, IT'S TIME TO MAKE A MOVE

Are you living in reactionary mode?

Reactionary living has no real destination. It causes you to live in response mode—something happens, and you respond. You have no real commitment that anchors you because something may always come up. You talk about your dreams and goals, but there's no substance behind them. You give them no start date and no end date. You're just responding to life as things come up, without really setting your life on any specific course. Are you living that way?

> "The plans of the diligent lead to profit as surely as haste leads to poverty." (Proverbs 21:5, NIV)

If so, what if you decided to get intentional about your life? Where would your life be? How different would your life be one year from now? How different would it be 30 days from now if you truly made today your day one of being intentional about your living?

What if you stopped just reacting and responding to whatever comes your way and instead charted your course? What if you decided the direction you want to go and took a chance on the things that have been in your heart? What would your life look like then? How would you wake up? Would you wake up with excitement, ready to take on the day because you had a plan and were eager to see it through? How different would your life be?

QUIET GIRL SZN

QUIET TIME

What steps can you take today to move from reactionary living to intentional living, and how might that change your life in the coming weeks and months?

PRAYER

Lord, help me to live intentionally, setting a course for my life that aligns with Your will, rather than simply reacting to whatever comes my way. In Jesus' name, Amen.

DAY **36**

GIRL, GET OUT OF YOUR WAY

Sometimes the person standing in your way is you. Many of the obstacles you've placed in your way are imaginary. Sometimes there are no real obstacles except for the stories you've told yourself—stories that consist of a bunch of what-ifs. We often play these scenarios out in our minds, going through the whole process as if they have actually happened, but they haven't. They're not even real. We've conjured up things in our minds and then allowed those things to let fear creep in. And when fear is crouching at your door, doubt soon follows.

"I can do all this through him who gives me strength." (Philippians 4:13, NIV)

Sometimes, you have to take a step back and look at the things you've been talking yourself out of. If you make up your mind to do something, you can do it. There's something amazing about determination, when you are determined and have made up your mind, you can accomplish anything. Determination won't let anything stand in your way and when you become clear about where you want to go and what you want to do things begin to change.

So instead of talking yourself out of things, allow determination to take the front seat and drive you to where you want to go.

QUIET TIME

What imaginary obstacles have you placed in your path, and how can you let determination guide you to overcome them?

PRAYER

Lord, help me to recognize when I am standing in my own way and give me the determination to push past fear and doubt, trusting in Your strength. In Jesus' name, Amen.

DAY 37

GIRL, PREPARE FOR WHAT YOU WANT

Are you asking for more? Can you be trusted with the little things? So often, we find ourselves wanting more; we desire bigger and better opportunities, blessings, and possessions. But before we step into those dreams, take a moment to reflect on how you are handling what you already have. It's easy to get caught up in the excitement of what's to come, but growth begins with stewardship. How are you managing the things currently in your life—the things already entrusted to you? It's in the small, everyday moments that we show our readiness for the next level. We may long for new blessings, but the real question is, can we be trusted with what we currently have?

"Whoever can be trusted with very little can also be trusted with much, and whoever is dishonest with very little will also be dishonest with much."
(Luke 16:10, NIV)

If you're asking for a bigger house, how are you taking care of your current living space? If you want new furniture, how are you maintaining the old? If you're asking for a new car, are you keeping your current car clean and well-maintained? The principle of stewardship shows us that how we handle the "little" things in our lives reflects how we will handle greater responsibilities and blessings.

Being a good steward is not just about material possessions; it applies to relationships, opportunities, and even time. If we desire more in any area of life, we must first honor what we already have. Stewardship is preparation for more. When God sees us managing what we have well, He knows we are ready for what's next. We must ask ourselves: Why would I receive more when I haven't shown I can handle what I already have?

QUIET TIME

How are you currently stewarding the things in your life, and what changes can you make to better prepare for what you're asking God for?

PRAYER

Lord, help me to be a good steward of what You've entrusted to me, so that I may be ready to receive more and handle it with wisdom and care. In Jesus' name, Amen.

DAY 38

GIRL, BELIEVE IN YOURSELF

Did you know you can do whatever you put your mind to? All you have to do is believe that you can. Your belief will take you further than you could ever imagine; it will open doors to places you never thought you could go. Sometimes, when you look at your circumstances, your upbringing, or the challenges you've been through, you might convince yourself that success, fulfillment, or breakthrough isn't meant for you. But that's a lie.

The mere fact that a dream or desire is in your heart is evidence that it could be for you. It's as if the dream was placed there by God Himself. The things you desire; those dreams and ambitions; are calling you to take action. They're not there by accident. Your desires are an invitation from God to step into a greater level of faith, trust, and belief in what He can do in your life.

> "'If you can'?" said Jesus. "Everything is possible for one who believes." (Mark 9:23, NIV)

Sometimes, the path to achieving your dreams seems unclear or too difficult. You might think, "I don't know if I can do this. It seems so far out of reach." But if you believe, if you trust in God and start taking action; even in the small steps, He will guide you. God has a way of opening doors that seemed locked and making paths where there were none. He places the right people in your life and arranges circumstances to lead you in the direction of your dreams.

You'll be amazed at what you can do when you choose to believe and trust in the possibilities that God has for you.

QUIET TIME

What desires are in your heart that you've been hesitant to pursue, and how can you start taking steps toward them with faith and belief?

PRAYER

Lord, help me to believe in the possibilities You've placed in my heart and to trust that You will guide me as I take steps toward fulfilling them. Strengthen my faith, so I may overcome doubt and move confidently toward the plans You have for me. In Jesus' name, Amen.

DAY 39

GIRL, ENCOURAGE YOURSELF

Do you ever have conversations with yourself?

Sometimes you just have to talk to yourself, to encourage yourself. I know a lot of people use affirmations, speaking words that uplift and inspire them. Sometimes, you have to do that too. I speak to myself all the time. I record voice notes to myself and often find them a year later, right at the moment when I need them. Words are powerful.

Be the woman God called you to be. Be brave. Be bold. Be fearless. Be faithful. Know that you were chosen by God. Lean into what He has called you to do, and do it the way He has called you to do it. Move with grace and excellence. Act with kindness and love. Know that God has already gone before you and prepared a place for you. All you have to do is walk it out. All you have to do is own it.

> *"So do not fear, for I am with you; do not be dismayed, for I am your God. I will strengthen you and help you; I will uphold you with my righteous right hand." (Isaiah 41:10, NIV)*

Encourage yourself, speak kind words to yourself, and be good to yourself. You are worth it. Your life is worth it. I want you to take a pause, stand in that truth, step into it, believe it, and receive it. Let something rise up inside you that says, "I can do this, I am brave." Believe it and speak with all the conviction you can muster. Sometimes, you just have to encourage yourself.

QUIET TIME

How can you make self-encouragement a daily habit, speaking life and truth over yourself?

PRAYER

Lord, help me to speak words of encouragement and truth over myself, reminding me of who You've called me to be. In Jesus' name, Amen.

DAY 40

GIRL, DON'T BE A QUITTER

Don't be a quitter. Put action behind your intentions, even when it feels hard. I know that sometimes things are not always going to work out the way you think they should, and it's okay if one thing doesn't work—you can try something else. But don't be a quitter. When I say don't be a quitter, I'm talking about intentionally giving up on things because they get hard, instead of recognizing when something just needs a different perspective, an adjustment, or some outside help.

If you go around quitting everything, when will you finish anything? And when I say don't be a quitter, that doesn't mean you can't stop something that isn't working or that you are no longer passionate about. It simply means don't keep quitting just because it gets hard. If you stay in it long enough, there is a point of breakthrough that happens when you push past a certain level of resistance. That resistance has to break.

> *"Let us not become weary in doing good, for at the proper time we will reap a harvest if we do not give up." (Galatians 6:9, NIV)*

But so often, we never stay in it long enough to reach that point of resistance. You have to stay in it until you reach that breaking point. On the other side of that is where you find victory. Many times we never get to the other side because as soon as we hit a brick wall, we quit. You don't realize that brick wall only has the appearance of being impenetrable. You can push past it, and even if you have to take it down brick by brick, there is something on the other side.

Just think about that. Every brick wall you see is there for a reason. It's either keeping something out or preventing something from getting in, which is a clear indication that there is something on the other side. What you want is to be able to get to the other side.

QUIET GIRL SZN

QUIET TIME

What brick wall are you facing in your life, and how can you push past it instead of giving up?

PRAYER

Lord, give me the strength to persevere through challenges and not give up when things get hard, knowing that there is victory on the other side. In Jesus' name, Amen.

DAY 41

GIRL, FOCUS!

Focus is going to take you really, really far. I was talking to someone the other day, and they were telling me about all the things they wanted to do, and they all sounded really, really great. But one of the things I had to let her know is that, yes, you can do all those things—you just can't do them all at once because they were all major things she wanted to accomplish.

I want you to think of focus as having one arrow and one bullseye, but multiple targets on the board. You can only hit one. What are you going to aim at? If you try aiming at all three, you'll hit nothing because you're not focusing. You're going back and forth. That's how I want you to look at life—look at the things you want to achieve.

> *"Brothers and sisters, I do not consider myself yet to have taken hold of it. But one thing I do: Forgetting what is behind and straining toward what is ahead, I press on toward the goal to win the prize for which God has called me heavenward in Christ Jesus." (Philippians 3:13-14, NIV)*

You have to be able to focus. My recommendation is that you focus on one thing at a time. See that thing to completion, and then, once you complete it, you can move on to the next thing. If you look at your life and realize that you are all over the place, check your focus. Are you giving a little bit to this, a little bit to that, and a little bit to something else? If you see that you're doing that, consider stopping spreading your efforts and focus on one thing. You'll see the difference. You'll start to achieve things faster, and you'll develop a sense of confidence in your ability to accomplish your goals.

QUIET GIRL SZN

QUIET TIME

What is one goal you can focus on exclusively to see it through to completion, and how can you eliminate distractions to achieve it?

PRAYER

Lord, help me to focus on the tasks and goals that You have set before me, guiding me to complete them with diligence and purpose. In Jesus' name, Amen.

DAY 42

GIRL, WHAT'S YOUR MOTIVE?

What's your motive?

Sometimes, we do things without fully considering why. Maybe we seek recognition or approval. Perhaps we act out of obligation because others expect it of us, or because it seems like what we should be doing. But have you ever stopped to ask yourself, Why am I really doing this? What's the driving force behind my actions? Motives matter.

They reveal the intentions of our hearts, just like in investigations where the motive behind a crime helps uncover the truth. In life, our motives drive our actions and define the spirit in which we do things. God knows the heart of everything we do, even when our outward actions seem pure. He looks at why we do what we do, and whether our hearts are aligned with His purpose.

> "All a person's ways seem pure to them, but motives are weighed by the Lord." (Proverbs 16:2, NIV)

Hidden motives can cloud our judgment. But when we take a moment to pause, reflect, and ask God to help us examine our motives, we gain clarity. Are you doing something because it's truly meaningful to you and aligns with God's plan? Or is it to fulfill external pressures, expectations, or for self-gain? It's crucial to make sure that what you're doing is born out of a pure motive, one that is aligned with God's will and direction for your life.

QUIET TIME

What are the motives behind your current actions, and how can you ensure they align with God's will for your life?

PRAYER

Lord, help me to examine my motives and purify them so that my actions align with Your will and purpose for my life. Lead me in integrity and truth as I walk out the plans You have for me. In Jesus' name, Amen.

DAY 43

GIRL, TAKE A MOMENT TO REFLECT

Self-examination and self-reflection are what's going to help you grow. Growth comes through taking a step back and really looking at where you are in life. Self-examination allows you to assess what's working and what isn't. It's in those moments of reflection that you can begin to extract the lessons that life has been trying to teach you. These lessons give you the wisdom to release what no longer serves you and embrace what is meant to elevate you to the next level. It's a way of shedding the things that weigh you down so you can freely move forward with clarity and purpose.

When you pause and look at your past decisions, you start to realize how they've shaped where you are today. You might say, "I don't live with regrets," and that's fine. But upon reflection, there may be areas where you could've handled things differently, with more wisdom or grace. That's the beauty of self-reflection: it gives you a chance to recalibrate and grow, learning from what has passed to create a better future.

"Examine yourselves to see whether you are in the faith; test yourselves. Do you not realize that Christ Jesus is in you—unless, of course, you fail the test?" (2 Corinthians 13:5, NIV)

Looking at life through the lens of faith and how Christ sees you allows you to approach every decision with divine wisdom and love. It's not about perfection, but about progress and about learning from each step, mistake, or triumph, and using those insights to align yourself more closely with God's purpose. Everything you do or don't do matters, and every moment can be a stepping stone toward a life that reflects the love and purpose of Christ.

QUIET TIME

What areas of your life need self-examination and reflection, and how can you use that insight to make better choices moving forward?

PRAYER

Lord, help me to examine my life with honesty and humility, allowing Your wisdom to guide my decisions so that I may grow and live according to Your purpose. In Jesus' name, Amen.

DAY 44

GIRL, REKINDLE THAT DREAM

Have you ever rediscovered a dream that was in your heart?

Maybe someone said something to you, or you read something you wrote, or perhaps a thought just popped into your mind, bringing back the memory of something you desired long ago. I want you to think about those deferred dreams. Langston Hughes wrote a poem about how a dream deferred makes the heart sick, and I want you to rekindle that dream—especially if, when you think about it, it makes you smile and fills you with a sense of possibility.

If thinking about that dream brings you joy, then it's time to rekindle it. Even if it's been long past and you've told yourself it could never be, what if you allowed yourself to reimagine that it could be? What if you allowed yourself to rethink a strategy to bring it to fruition? Don't let the dream die in you just because you don't know how.

> *"Commit to the Lord whatever you do,
> and he will establish your plans."*
> *(Proverbs 16:3, NIV)*

The "how" isn't the important part; the important part is the decision to go after it. When you decide and commit to going after it, you'll be amazed at how the "how" will start to appear. You'll begin to see things that line up with the dream. People will come into your life that align with the dream. Don't get caught up on the "how." I want to invite you to revisit that long-lost dream and go for it.

QUIET TIME

What dream have you deferred that brings you joy when you think about it, and how can you start taking steps to rekindle that dream today?

PRAYER

Lord, help me to revisit the dreams You've placed in my heart, trusting that as I commit them to You, You will guide my steps and bring them to fruition. In Jesus' name, Amen.

DAY 45

GIRL, KEEP YOUR EYES ON GOD

Don't take your eyes off God, because that is where your help comes from. I know that sometimes in life, circumstances can rock us to the core. There may be a loss of a job, a loss of a home, a divorce, or the loss of a loved one. In those moments, it can be hard to see how we'll ever come out of it. It feels so overwhelming and painful, but I want to invite you to always keep your eyes on God, no matter what's going on. He always has your answers. There is always comfort in Him, even when you're in the midst of it and can't see a way out.

When life gets hard, it's easy to lose focus, but it's in these times that we need to hold on to God's promises. It may not be immediately clear how God is working in your situation, but He is. Remember, He is not just the God of your mountaintops but also the God of your valleys. In the darkest moments, His light shines brightest. And it's often when we're looking back that we can truly see how God was orchestrating everything for our good.

> "I lift up my eyes to the mountains—where does my help come from? My help comes from the Lord, the Maker of heaven and earth." (Psalm 121:1-2, NIV)

I want you to remember this for the next time, because there will be other times and other challenges. In this life, we are going to face troubles, but we don't have to be discouraged by them. God has already taken control of them. If we trust Him to lead us and guide us, He'll show us the way.

He'll make our crooked places straight. He'll illuminate our dark places. He'll show us the path to take when we come to a fork in the road. Don't be discouraged. Keep your eyes on God.

QUIET TIME

What situation in your life right now requires you to keep your eyes on God, trusting Him to guide you through?

PRAYER

Lord, help me to keep my eyes fixed on You, trusting that You are my source of help and strength in every situation. In Jesus' name, Amen.

DAY 46

GIRL, IT'S NEXT LEVEL

Your next level is going to require a new version of you.

What used to work on one level is not going to be sufficient for the next level. You'll take the lessons you've learned throughout your life and use them to propel you forward, but it's going to require you to think higher, think bigger, and think more of yourself in order to reach this new version of you and the next level of your life.

If you want more in life, you're going to have to do more. More will be required of you—you'll need to think differently, talk differently, and even walk differently. Sometimes, your environment may need to change. You may need to adjust your social circle or avoid places that are no longer conducive to the life you want to live and the level you want to reach.

> *"See, I am doing a new thing! Now it springs up; do you not perceive it? I am making a way in the wilderness and streams in the wasteland." (Isaiah 43:19, NIV)*

Think about how you dress for the beach versus how you dress for a restaurant—it's two different things. You have to think about where you're going and dress for the occasion. The same principle applies to your mindset. Preparation is key to moving to the next level. So, consider where you're aiming to go and what preparation is necessary to get there. What do you need to stop doing, and what are some things you need to start doing?

QUIET TIME

What changes and preparations do you need to make in your life to reach the next level, and how can you begin implementing them today?

PRAYER

Lord, help me to embrace the changes and preparations needed to reach the next level You have for me. Guide me in thinking higher, acting with purpose, and stepping into the new version of myself. In Jesus' name, Amen.

DAY 47

GIRL, JUMP!

Sometimes you just have to take a step of faith, not knowing where it's going to lead you or how it's going to turn out. Otherwise, you might find yourself going around in circles, like the Israelites who wandered in the desert for 40 years. Sometimes you just have to make a decision, like when you're preparing to jump into a double Dutch rope. You're rocking back and forth, looking for the right moment to jump in, but sometimes things aren't always going to line up perfectly the way you want them to.

"For we live by faith, not by sight."
(2 Corinthians 5:7, NIV)

When you take that step of faith, even with the uncertainty ahead, you're positioning yourself for growth and discovery. Waiting for everything to fall perfectly into place can sometimes be an excuse to stay in our comfort zone. It's in those moments of trust—when we take a leap despite our doubts—that God can truly show us His power, His provision, and His guidance. Faith isn't just about knowing the outcome; it's about trusting that God is with you through the unknown, guiding your steps even when you can't see the whole path.

You may need to reposition some things. You may need to fix some things along the way, but you won't know what you need until you step out. Sometimes you have to take that step of faith and believe that it will work out, being courageous enough to say, "I don't know where this is leading me, but I'm willing to find out." In doing so, you discover a lot more than you expected. You discover new things and learn things about yourself that you never knew you could do, and that in itself makes the leap worth it.

QUIET TIME

What leap of faith have you been hesitating to take, and how can you trust God to guide you through the unknown?

PRAYER

Lord, give me the courage to take a leap of faith, trusting that You will guide me through the unknown and reveal new strengths and opportunities along the way. In Jesus' name, Amen.

DAY 48

GIRL, YOU ARE A GIFT

Do you know that your life is necessary, purposeful, and that someone is waiting for you?

You should consider spending your life doing good—not just for yourself, but for the greater good of it all. You should enjoy your life. You should live the life that you want to live, and you should be good to people, knowing that you have been given such a gift in life. You are a gift to this earth and to this world. We used to joke and say, "Oh, I'm God's greatest gift," but in reality, we truly are.

> "For I know the plans I have for you," declares the Lord, "plans to prosper you and not to harm you, plans to give you hope and a future."
> (Jeremiah 29:11, NIV)

Think about how you view yourself. Do you see yourself as a gift? Do you see your life as necessary? Or are you simply going through the motions, thinking that you're just existing, taking up space, going to work, and doing what you do without any great significance? The significance is *you*. You are significant. And when you start to see your life that way, when you recognize that you matter, you'll live differently. You'll see things differently.

Your life is not an accident; it has meaning. God designed you with a purpose in mind, and the fact that you are here at this moment means you have a unique contribution to make to the world. It could be a kind word to someone in need, a talent you haven't fully explored, or a calling you've felt but haven't acted on yet. Know that there is a divine assignment connected to your life, and someone out there is waiting for what only you can bring. Embrace your significance and allow yourself to be used for the good God intended.

QUIET GIRL SZN

QUIET TIME

How can you begin to see your life as significant and purposeful, and what steps can you take to live with that awareness?

PRAYER

Lord, help me to see my life as a gift and to recognize the significance You have placed within me. Guide me to live with purpose, knowing that my life matters. In Jesus' name, Amen.

DAY 49

GIRL, PRAYER CHANGES THINGS

Did you pray about it?

I know you might ask, "Pray about what?" Pray about whatever is on your heart. When you have decisions to make, when things aren't going the way you thought they should, when everything and everyone around you seems out of whack, when you feel overwhelmed with so many decisions, when you don't know your next move or what to do or say—did you pray about it?

Prayer is one of the greatest gifts that God gave us. It's the entry point for Him to speak into our lives. It's how we give Him access because we have free will, and He won't intrude on our lives. Prayer is saying, "God, I invite You into this situation. I invite You into my life because I don't know what to do. The kids are acting crazy, the husband is wilding out, my job is getting on my nerves. I don't know what's going on, but everything around me has me feeling anxious and depressed, and I don't know what to do about it."

> *"Do not be anxious about anything, but in every situation, by prayer and petition, with thanksgiving, present your requests to God. And the peace of God, which transcends all understanding, will guard your hearts and your minds in Christ Jesus." (Philippians 4:6-7, NIV)*

Pray about it. It doesn't matter what is going on in your life; God is concerned about every area. It doesn't matter what it is. If you broke a nail and it hurts, God is concerned. That's the level of care I want you to understand—how deeply God is ingrained in your life, down to the minute details. If He knows every single hair on your head, do you think He is not concerned about you?

QUIET TIME

What situation in your life do you need to pray about today, inviting God into the details?

PRAYER

Lord, remind me to bring every concern to You in prayer, trusting that You care about every detail of my life and that You will provide the peace I need. In Jesus' name, Amen.

DAY 50

GIRL, STOP THE SABOTAGE

I think sometimes I used to secretly search out problems.

If there was a good day going on, I couldn't just enjoy it. I felt like, "Hmm, this is too good to be true," so I started searching, seeking, looking for trouble. And when you search and seek for things, whatever you are looking for, you will find it. Dig long enough and deep enough, and you'll find it. What I didn't realize was that I was secretly sabotaging myself. I couldn't believe that good things would happen to me because of all the past traumas in my life. I wasn't able to receive the good. So if there was a good day, it felt uneasy to me. Do you ever feel like that?

"You will keep in perfect peace those whose minds are steadfast, because they trust in you."
(Isaiah 26:3, NIV)

Do you ever feel like there's always a calm before the storm and you're just waiting for the other shoe to drop? That's not a way to live. Life is a journey, and it is meant to be enjoyed. You don't have to look for the bad in everything. You can find joy in the journey and live through that. Don't sabotage yourself or look for ways to disturb your peace. When you have those peaceful moments, receive them. Because on the other side of that, sometimes, there could be other things lurking, but in those moments, enjoy where you are and receive the peace that passes all understanding.

Part of the reason many of us find it hard to accept peace is because we've conditioned ourselves to expect the worst. Whether it's past trauma, fear of disappointment, or a cycle of negativity, it's easy to believe that peace won't last. But we can choose to trust in God's plan for our lives. His peace is different from anything this world offers—it's steady, lasting, and doesn't depend on circumstances. By trusting in Him, we allow ourselves to receive the good moments and stop sabotaging them with our fears. Remember, peace is not the absence of challenges, but the presence of God in the midst of it all.

QUIET GIRL SZN

QUIET TIME

Are you sabotaging your peace by searching for problems? How can you learn to fully receive and enjoy the good moments in your life?

PRAYER

Lord, help me to trust in Your peace and embrace the good moments in my life without fear or sabotage. Teach me to find joy in the journey and to rest in the peace You provide. In Jesus' name, Amen.

DAY 51

GIRL, EVERYTHING DON'T HAVE TO BE HARD

Everything doesn't always have to be so hard. I think sometimes we believe that things have to be hard for them to be fruitful or meaningful because we've become accustomed to the struggle. But sometimes, some things aren't hard, and we can experience those pockets of life that are easy. Like the Staples "easy button," we wish we could press a button and it be that easy. Like if we could command the wind in our faces on a hot summer day. Have you ever caught a good cool breeze of air in the heat, it so refreshing.

Everything doesn't have to be hard. When you get those easy days, embrace them. Not everything requires gut-wrenching effort. Not everything is going to require a sledgehammer. Some things will give way with just a push of your finger, and you realize, "Oh, okay. That wasn't as bad as I thought it would be."

When those moments come receive them.

> *"The Lord is my shepherd, I lack nothing. He makes me lie down in green pastures, he leads me beside quiet waters, he refreshes my soul." (Psalm 23:1-2, NIV)*

Receive this "softer era" in your life. There's a beauty in it. So I guess we can embrace the new "soft girl" era. But you get to define what it means to you and for you. Remember that God gives us grace and mercy that are renewed daily and it's not just an era, it's for a lifetime.

QUIET TIME

Are you allowing yourself to experience the easier moments in life, or do you feel like everything has to be hard? How can you embrace a "softer era" in your life?

PRAYER

Lord, help me to recognize and embrace the easier moments in life, trusting that not everything has to be hard. Lead me beside quiet waters and refresh my soul, as I learn to rest in Your peace. In Jesus' name, Amen.

DAY 52

GIRL, STEAL AWAY

When was the last time you got away? Like, just for no reason—just you, all by yourself—where you had a moment to really assess life, where you got a chance to just be with yourself? A moment where you could simply think, process, and envision. Have you ever had a moment like that?

> *"Then, because so many people were coming and going that they did not even have a chance to eat, he said to them, 'Come with me by yourselves to a quiet place and get some rest.'" (Mark 6:31, NIV)*

Periodically, I've checked into a hotel, usually at the beginning of the year, to cast a vision for what I want to do in my life and business. There's no TV; it's just God, my thoughts, and my notes. I put paper all over the walls to draw and write out my ideas. It's uninterrupted time, something I could never do at home because there are always people and things around me. Sometimes you need to steal away to a new place to gain new insights, new perspectives, and new visions.

If you've never done that, I want to invite you to do it. Take a moment to steal away with just you, God, your dreams, your goals, and your hopes. Take time to live in that, relish it, and see what greatness you can conjure up.

QUIET TIME

When was the last time you took intentional time away to reflect, dream, and envision your future? How can you create space for that in your life?

PRAYER

Lord, help me to find time to steal away and be with You, to reflect on my life and dreams. Grant me new insights and visions as I seek Your guidance for my future. In Jesus' name, Amen.

DAY 53

GIRL, STOP DREAMING AND START DOING

Have you ever found yourself thinking about all the things you want to do?

You've even gone so far as to write them down, telling anyone who will listen, talking about them. But the one thing you haven't done is put any real intention behind them. Sometimes, part of the reason why is that we struggle with the belief that it could really happen for us.

I remember doing all those things. I would dream about it, I would think about it, I would talk about it. I would write them down. All of my journal notes had them all in it. But the one thing that was missing was the action. I wasn't putting any work behind them because, secretly, I didn't know if it would work. I didn't know how to bring them to pass. I didn't know what to do. So, I think I had relegated myself to just the continual dreaming and writing because, at least that way, it was enough to keep the dream alive.

> *"In the same way, faith by itself, if it is not accompanied by action, is dead." (James 2:17, NIV)*

But then I realized I didn't want to just keep it alive. I realized that the days of our lives are ticking away, passing us by. And I really wanted to put real action behind it. So, I started taking action. And when I did, amazing things started to happen.

What are you waiting for?

QUIET TIME

What dreams have you been thinking about and talking about, but haven't taken action on? How can you start putting your faith into action today?

PRAYER

Lord, help me to move from dreaming and talking about my goals to taking real action. Give me the courage and wisdom to step out in faith, trusting that You will guide me as I work toward bringing them to pass. In Jesus' name, Amen.

DAY 54

GIRL, STOP BEING SO BUSY

Are you available, or are you too busy?

If God was looking for someone to use, could He call you? Would you pick up the phone? I always see those memes where it shows a phone screen with "God is calling," and there's a yes or no button to answer. That's just the physical representation, and we share it and send it around. But I want you to really think about that. If God was calling you, would you send Him to voicemail?

"Then I heard the voice of the Lord saying, 'Whom shall I send? And who will go for us?' And I said, 'Here am I. Send me!'"
(Isaiah 6:8, NIV)

Is your phone on "Do Not Disturb"? Are you available? So many times, we say we want God to use us, or we want to do amazing and extraordinary things with our lives, but for whose glory? Are the things you want to do self-seeking and self-serving? Can God use you? Will you say yes? Will you answer the call and allow Him to lead you, even if you don't know where it will take you, but trust that if God is leading, it's going to be good?

Sometimes, we desire greatness and purpose, but our lives are so cluttered with distractions that when God calls, we can't hear Him. Being available for God doesn't mean living in a constant state of busyness or always saying yes to everything around you. It means having room in your heart, your schedule, and your life for God's direction. It means positioning yourself to listen, to be willing, and to act on what He's calling you to do. He's not looking for perfection, just an open heart ready to say, "Here I am. Send me."

QUIET GIRL SZN

QUIET TIME

Are you truly available for God to use you, or are you too busy with your own plans? How can you make yourself more available to answer His call?

PRAYER

Lord, help me to be available and willing to answer your call. Remove any distractions or self-seeking desires that keep me from being fully committed to your purpose for my life. In Jesus' name, Amen.

DAY 55

GIRL, ARE YOU MAKING AN IMPACT?

When my aunt passed away, I had the pleasure of reading her obituary. She was such a major force in my life. She took me in when I didn't have anywhere to go, especially when I was younger and my mom would put me out for not following her rules. I only understand this now as an adult, but when I was younger, I couldn't comprehend why my mom would put me out—who puts their child out? But my aunt would always take me in and make me feel at home. When she passed, she was the first person in my life whose death had a profound impact on me. She saved me from so many situations, and I felt her love for me was unconditional. In her death, I was given two words: moments and impact. I even talked about them at her funeral.

> "In the same way, let your light shine before others, that they may see your good deeds and glorify your Father in heaven." (Proverbs 27:17, NIV)

You never know when someone will enter your life and create moments that can forever change you. We have to be present enough to receive those moments. There are people who come into our lives who have a significant impact on who we are as individuals. I'll never forget her, and I'll never forget to live in the moments and always strive to make an impact. I want you to do the same. Cherish those moments, and think about how you can make an impact on someone's life.

QUIET TIME

Who in your life has made a significant impact, and how can you honor their legacy by making a positive impact on others?

PRAYER

Lord, help me to cherish the moments and the people who have shaped my life. Guide me to be a source of light and impact in the lives of others. In Jesus' name, Amen.

DAY 56
GIRL, DON'T MAKE A DECISION ALONE

Do you ever get stumped on a decision about what to do? Not only about what to do, but sometimes decisions are hard, and it takes courage to carry them out. Asking God for wisdom to make the right decision is what will set you apart from someone who just makes a decision without seeking guidance.

I went to the doctor the other day, and we were discussing some options. She gave me choices and asked if I wanted to proceed, and I said, "Well, I need to think about it." I also mentioned that I needed to talk to my husband about it and pray about it. She responded with, "Yes, pray about it. That's good."

It was the way she said it—there was a pause, probably because she isn't accustomed to people saying, "Let me pray about it." I don't want to make decisions without God because I'm not as smart as I think I am. Sometimes, I tell myself that I am smart, and while I may be smart about some things, I'm not smart about everything—especially the decisions that truly matter in my life. I need God's wisdom to help me make decisions so that I'm not just acting on my own limited knowledge.

> "Trust in the Lord with all your heart and lean not on your own understanding; in all your ways submit to him, and he will make your paths straight." (Proverbs 3:5-6, NIV)

God sees all and knows all; He knows the plans He has for you. Ask Him to give you peace about whatever decision you are making, so you know that you have gone to the source, and it's not just you out here on your own. So when it comes time to make decisions, add God into the equation from the beginning and allow Him to lead and guide you. I will always stand by the advice to allow God to guide you in your decision-making process in every single area of your life. If it concerns you, it concerns God.

QUIET GIRL SZN

QUIET TIME

What decision are you facing right now that you need to bring before God, and how can you seek His wisdom and peace before moving forward?

PRAYER

Lord, I ask for Your wisdom in every decision I make. Help me to trust in Your guidance and not rely solely on my own understanding. Lead me to make choices that align with Your will and bring peace to my heart. In Jesus' name, Amen.

DAY 57

GIRL, IT MAY BE A TRUST THING

Who's in your life? Who is in your circle of people? Or do you even have a circle? Sometimes I joke and say I don't have a circle—I have a bend. But it's interesting because I hear a lot of people saying they don't really have people in their lives like that. I realize that, often, when we don't have people in our lives, it's a trust issue. We've been betrayed, and we don't trust easily.

To have a circle of people in your life—when I say circle, I'm not just talking about acquaintances, but that close circle of people who can serve in your life in different ways and whom you can serve in theirs. They can be your confidants, the ones you share your deepest thoughts with. Do you have people with whom you can have deep conversations, or do you only have surface-level conversations?

> "Two are better than one, because they have a good return for their labor: If either of them falls down, one can help the other up. But pity anyone who falls and has no one to help them up." (Ecclesiastes 4:9-10, NIV)

We have all different types of people in our lives. There are people we hang out with, people we have fun with, people we may go to church with. We have different types of relationships, and different people in our lives serve different purposes. But the relationships I want to focus on are the ones with deep connections—you don't need many of those. If you have one or two people you truly trust, who are a safe and soft place to land when life gets hard, that's a blessing.

Consider who is in your life. Examine your group of friends. They may not even be friends; it could be a family member, a spouse, a sibling. But who is your soft place to land? And if you don't have one, I want you to ask yourself why. Why don't you trust enough to share the deep things in life?

QUIET TIME

Who in your life is your safe place to land, and if you don't have one, what steps can you take to build deeper, more trusting relationships?

PRAYER

Lord, help me to build and nurture deep, trusting relationships with those You have placed in my life. Open my heart to trust others and to be a safe place for them as well. In Jesus' name, Amen.

DAY 58

GIRL, PICK UP A BOOK

Besides this devotional that you're reading, do you read books? I remember I used to avoid reading books, especially as I entered adulthood. Coming out of school, we were required to read books and write book reports, and most of us hated it. There were some bookworms who really loved it, but I wasn't one of them. But it wasn't until I got older and wanted to change my life that I started reading and seeking other perspectives.

In life, you only know what you know. You only know what's within your immediate surroundings. You only know the things you see, but when you read something, you gain another perspective. You enter the mind of someone else and learn how they think.

> "The heart of the discerning acquires knowledge, for the ears of the wise seek it out."
> (Proverbs 18:15, NIV)

When I started reading, my world began to open up. I started to see things I had never seen before and think about things I had never considered. Now, I enjoy reading. There was a book that actually started as a devotional called *Women on the Front Lines: A Call to Courage.* I got a snippet of it, and it said if you want more, visit a certain website. I visited the website and found out that there was a whole book, so I got the book.

When I tell you that book changed my life—it truly did. The stories of women and their courage to be who they were called to be were inspiring. I don't think they realized it in those moments as they lived their lives, but reading their stories revealed the courage they had. Sometimes we just do things without recognizing the bravery it takes, but in

DAY 58

hindsight, or when someone reads the story, the courage becomes evident.

So, if you don't read books, I want to encourage you to start. And you don't even have to physically read them—you can listen to books now. Reading (or listening) will change your life. It will broaden your perspective and open you up to more possibilities. When you see others who have gone before you standing in their courage, it gives you the courage to be courageous.

QUIET TIME

What book has had a significant impact on your life, or what book could you start reading to gain new perspectives and courage?

PRAYER

Lord, open my heart and mind to the knowledge and wisdom found in reading. Help me to find inspiration in the stories of others and to grow in courage as I seek to be who You've designed me to be. In Jesus' name, Amen.

DAY 59

GIRL LEAD WITH LOVE

Lead with love and give others grace. What do I mean by that? When you have the opportunity to either be mad and angry or lead with love, which one do you choose? Of course, you're not saying, "Well, I'd just rather be mad and angry." No one would rather be mad and angry. It's a natural emotion when things don't go the way we thought they should, or someone says something out of line, or someone does something that just goes too far. Love in that moment is not our first response, but it could be—and it takes practice.

So what does that look like? It looks like stopping for a minute and really opening up the level of communication, with clear understanding of what is actually happening. When you lead with love, it softens you and makes you more approachable, enabling you to hear better. Love is more graceful in those moments.

When I've read the scripture about love being patient and kind, I hear that, but as I continue reading, it also talks about how love bears all things.

> "Love is patient, love is kind. It does not envy, it does not boast, it is not proud. It does not dishonor others, it is not self-seeking, it is not easily angered, it keeps no record of wrongs. Love does not delight in evil but rejoices with the truth. It always protects, always trusts, always hopes, always perseveres." (1 Corinthians 13:4-7, NIV)

And that's what we need during these times. We need to be able to bear it. It talks about how love endures all things and is not irritable. So, when you get an opportunity to think about how you are going to respond, choose to respond in love, even when it's not your first choice, even when the situation is difficult. If you can view it through the lens of love, you'll be able to maneuver differently. God can soften your heart so that you can see things more clearly, and He can use you in an amazing way to bring peace, harmony, and reconciliation to a circumstance.

QUIET GIRL SZN

QUIET TIME

In what situations do you find it difficult to lead with love, and how can you practice responding with grace instead of anger?

PRAYER

Lord, help me to lead with love and give others grace, especially in challenging situations. Soften my heart and guide my responses so that I can bring peace and understanding wherever I go. In Jesus' name, Amen.

DAY 60

GIRL, DO YOU DREAM

Do you dream? I asked my husband one day if he dreams, and he told me he doesn't dream I don't know, maybe he just doesn't want to tell me, lol. I was thinking to myself, who doesn't dream? But then I realized that maybe everyone may not dream, or at least not everyone remembers their dreams. I also realized that I don't dream every night, and if I do, I don't always remember it. But there are times when I dream, and my dreams are so vivid, almost like in color, and they feel like real life. I also believe that my dreams mean something. I feel like they're messages from God, not just the result of what I ate for dinner. We often joke that our dreams are caused by the food we ate, but what does the food have to do with dreams? I never quite understood that.

Sometimes our dreams can be outlandish, and sometimes they seem to be all over the place. One of the things I've learned to do is when I dream—especially if it's a disturbing dream—I wake up and ask God, "What did that mean?" It's interesting that throughout the day or even in that moment, He will may reveal to me what the dream meant. It's fascinating to me how our dreams can play a role in our lives.

> *"For God does speak—now one way, now another—though no one perceives it. In a dream, in a vision of the night, when deep sleep falls on people as they slumber in their beds." (Job 33:14-15, NIV)*

Do you dream? And if you don't dream, ask God to start giving you dreams, because it could be His way of speaking to you. I believe God sometimes gives me messages in my dreams because I'm so busy during the day, running around. He's like, "Girl, I don't have time to tell you anything during the day. I'm going to have to catch you when you're asleep, when everything is shut down, and I'll give you a download."

But don't be that person who is so busy that God can't even get a message to you. God has something to say. Are we listening?

QUIET GIRL SZN

QUIET TIME

Do you pay attention to your dreams, and how can you be more intentional about asking God for understanding when you dream?

PRAYER

Lord, help me to be attentive to the dreams You give me and to seek Your guidance in understanding them. Keep my heart and mind open to the messages You want to share with me, even in the quiet moments of sleep. In Jesus' name, Amen.

DAY 61

GIRL, ARE YOU GROWING?

Do you know that life's challenges help you grow? It's not in the good times that we truly grow. It's in the dark times that our character is developed, and we discover what we are made of. It's when we have to make those hard choices, when we have to say the hard things—that's when we truly discover who we are. Life offers us these challenges to help us grow and move to the next level of what we have been called to do. Sometimes we want things, but we may not be ready for them. There are times when we need to mature and grow.

I remember when my youngest daughter wanted a car, and I was excited for her. I wanted to get her a car, but my husband said she wasn't ready. Even though she had her driver's license and was of age to drive, he felt that she wasn't ready maturity-wise. She was upset about it, but looking back, even in the days and weeks that followed, I got a chance to really see what he was talking about—she wasn't ready.

> "Consider it pure joy, my brothers and sisters, whenever you face trials of many kinds, because you know that the testing of your faith produces perseverance. Let perseverance finish its work so that you may be mature and complete, not lacking anything." (James 1:2-4, NIV)

Life has a way of showing you when you are ready for things and when you are not. Sometimes, it's in those adverse moments, in those unfavorable circumstances, that we get a chance to see what we're really made of. You know, they say pressure busts pipes, and the pressure of what's inside will come out. So when things get heated, when things get tough, you really see what you are made of.

I've learned to appreciate life's ups and downs—the highs, the lows, the valleys, and the mountains—because I realize that they are all weaving together something beautiful, something amazing. It's something in the making. And the making is you.

QUIET GIRL SZN

QUIET TIME

How have life's challenges helped you grow, and how can you embrace these moments as opportunities for growth rather than obstacles?

PRAYER

Lord, help me to see life's challenges as opportunities for growth and maturity. Strengthen my faith through trials, and guide me to become the person You are shaping me to be. In Jesus' name, Amen.

DAY 62

GIRL, DON'T CHASE THE WRONG THING

What if I told you that God didn't call you to be successful, but that He called you to be faithful, and that He will give you success?

What if I told you that you are striving for the wrong things? It's not about chasing after success, money, or being the next big thing. What if you were just called to be faithful with what you have and where you are? That should be your focus. When you allow faithfulness to be your focus, God can take care of all the other things in your life. He'll give you the desires of your heart, take you places you've wanted to go, and show you things you've wanted to see. All He requires is your faithfulness.

The world looks at success and status, but that's not what God looks at. God looks at your heart. Can you make faithfulness your barometer? Can you make faithfulness the meter by which you gauge how you're living your life and the things you're doing? Are you being faithful to what you are doing? Are you being faithful to what you have been given to be a steward over?

"His master replied, 'Well done, good and faithful servant! You have been faithful with a few things; I will put you in charge of many things. Come and share your master's happiness!'" (Matthew 25:21, NIV)

How are you handling that? What are you measuring it by? I get it—faithfulness on the surface doesn't seem glamorous, but it is everything. It is everything that you will need for your life. When the world gets too big, too noisy, and too loud, and you feel shut out and unseen, your faithfulness will be what keeps you and sustains you through it all. So if I had to choose between faithfulness and success, I would choose faithfulness every time. What will you choose?

QUIET GIRL SZN

QUIET TIME

Are you focusing on being faithful with what God has given you, or are you chasing after success as the world defines it? How can you shift your focus to faithfulness?

PRAYER

Lord, help me to prioritize faithfulness over worldly success. Teach me to be faithful with what You have entrusted to me, trusting that You will take care of the rest. In Jesus' name, Amen.

DAY 63

GIRL, IT'S NOT ALWAYS ABOUT YOU

Knowledge and awareness of self are so important. You can't try to change others to conform to a world that suits you, and you can't make it all about you and what you want. You have to respect and trust that just because others don't move the way you do, that doesn't make them wrong—they just do things differently. It's your responsibility to figure out ways to move in harmony with others, especially with people you have to work or interact with. Everyone doesn't see things the way you see them. We all have different lenses and perspectives, but the goal is to figure out how we can coexist and live in harmony with one another.

> "Live in harmony with one another. Do not be proud, but be willing to associate with people of low position. Do not be conceited." (Romans 12:16, NIV)

How can we respect another person's point of view without being angry that they don't see things the way we do? It's okay. There are so many things we can learn from people, even down to what not to do. People can teach us something. It's not about everyone knowing what you know or seeing what you see. It's about being self-aware enough to recognize, "This is what I bring to the table; this is who I am, and this is how I view things." But it's also about being open to hearing others' perspectives.

Ask, "Help me see what it is that you see so that I can broaden my horizons and understand where we are, so we can come to a mutual understanding." Sometimes that might involve compromising. It may not always be what you think it should be. Maybe you give a little, and the other person gives a little. But the goal is that both parties walk away feeling heard and seen. When you are aware of yourself, you don't always have to feel like it's all about you because you understand your purpose and perspective, knowing that all will be well.

QUIET TIME

How can you practice self-awareness and respect others' perspectives, even when they differ from your own? What steps can you take to create harmony in your relationships?

PRAYER

Lord, help me to grow in self-awareness and to respect the perspectives of others. Teach me to live in harmony with those around me, seeking mutual understanding and peace in all my relationships. In Jesus' name, Amen.

DAY 64

GIRL, IT'S UP TO YOU

One of the most powerful driving forces in your life is accountability. It's about owning your words, your actions, and your choices. Real growth happens when you take full responsibility for your life—when you stand in front of the mirror and say, "Okay, it's time to get it together. No more excuses. No more blaming anyone else."

Often, we live in denial about the things we avoid, the habits we cling to, and the decisions we keep putting off. We might point fingers at others, justifying our reactions to their actions, but here's the truth: no one can make you do anything. Your response is your responsibility, and that's where accountability starts.

"Whoever conceals their sins does not prosper, but the one who confesses and renounces them finds mercy." Proverbs 28:13 (NIV)

People may not always do what they're supposed to, and life might throw you curveballs, but you have the power to choose how you respond. If you don't hold yourself accountable, how will you grow? How will you break free from the cycle of stagnation?

If your life looks the same year after year, it's because you're making the same choices—or worse, not making any choices at all. And yes, not making a decision is a decision in itself. So today, I want to challenge you to step up. Own your part. Face the areas of your life where you've been passive, where you've avoided hard truths. Start making intentional decisions that align with the growth, purpose, and calling that God has for you.

It's time to get off the hamster wheel and live the life God has designed for you. Take that hard look in the mirror, speak the truth to yourself, and let it set you free.

QUIET GIRL SZN

QUIET TIME

What areas of your life have you been avoiding accountability in? What will you do differently starting today?

PRAYER

Lord, help me to see the areas of my life where I need to take ownership and accountability. Give me the strength and wisdom to make different decisions, ones that align with Your will and my purpose. Guide me to be honest with myself, and let Your truth set me free. In Jesus' name, Amen.

DAY 65

GIRL, WHERE YOU AT?

Take a moment to examine your life. I mean, really look at where you are versus where you thought you'd be. Are you living the life you've envisioned for yourself? And if the answer is no, ask yourself why. What paths have you chosen? Have you been settling, making excuses, or playing small? I want you to focus on your daily actions because they are what make up the sum of your life. Every day you either take steps forward, stand still, or even go backward.

What's driving you? Do you have a plan, a written-down set of goals, or do you wake up every day just waiting to see what happens? The truth is, without a vision, your days lack purpose. It's easy to feel like life is happening to you instead of you actively shaping your life. But here's the good news: you can change that by aligning your actions with your goals and by knowing the season you're in.

"There is a time for everything, and a season for every activity under the heavens." Ecclesiastes 3:1 (NIV)

Life flows in seasons. Some are for planting, some are for waiting, and others are for harvesting. What season are you in right now? Are you planting seeds of growth, ideas, and faith, or are you reaping the rewards of the hard work you've put in? And maybe you're in that often-overlooked waiting season—the season of quiet development where God is working behind the scenes.

Don't rush to get to the harvest. Development happens in the waiting. It's in this season that your character, patience, and faith are tested and strengthened. So often, we want the reward without the waiting, but the truth is that the waiting season prepares us for the harvest, ensuring we have the capacity to sustain the blessings coming our way.

QUIET TIME

What season of life are you currently in, and how are you preparing for what's next?

PRAYER

Lord, help me to discern the season I'm in and embrace it fully. Teach me to be patient in the waiting, diligent in the planting, and grateful in the harvest. Let my actions align with Your purpose for my life, and give me the wisdom to trust Your timing. In Jesus' name, Amen.

DAY 66

GIRL, IT'S TIME TO GET CLEAR

Gaining clarity is going to help you get so much insight into where you're looking to go in your life. It's going to be the deciding factor in whether or not you achieve and reach the pinnacles of what you've been striving for. When you have clarity, it means you're able to see clearly. When you create a vision for your life and gain clarity around that vision, it becomes the catalyst that propels you forward on this journey called life. But on the flip side, if you lack clarity, ask yourself if you've set a vision for your life.

We all know the phrase from Habakkuk 2:2, "Write the vision and make it plain." There's a reason for this—it helps us gain a clear vision and to write that vision down. It's like wanting to go somewhere, but the GPS is of no use if you don't give it a destination. Where do you want your life to go? Pay attention to your words because they will lead you in the direction of your life. Though invisible, your words are orchestrating your steps toward where you want to go.

> *"Where there is no vision, the people perish; but blessed is the one who heeds wisdom's instruction." (Proverbs 29:18, NIV)*

Take an assessment of your life to determine whether or not you have a vision. If you need to gain a vision for clarity, start by paying attention to your words. The words you speak will determine the steps you take in life. Don't worry about whether the vision seems possible or impossible, or what others might say or think, or what you have or don't have. Focus solely on the vision. When you do that and write the vision down, you'll be amazed at the clarity you gain about how to proceed and the next steps to take.

All because you decided to write down a vision, you were able to give your life direction. Without direction, your life will simply react to circumstances, leading to a reactionary existence. But with a vision, you give your life direction, and that makes all the difference. That's how you achieve clarity and vision for your life.

QUIET TIME

Have you taken the time to set a clear vision for your life, and how can writing it down help you gain the clarity needed to move forward?

PRAYER

Lord, help me to gain clarity and vision for my life. Guide me as I write down the vision You have for me, and lead my steps so that I can move forward with purpose and direction. In Jesus' name, Amen.

DAY 67

GIRL, CONFRONT YOUR FEARS

I realize that fear is always going to be present. I can't remember many times when fear wasn't present. It's something that, in life, we have allowed to consume us, and it has robbed us. Sometimes, it stops us from doing the things we want to do. We fear so many things, usually because it's fear of the unknown. We don't know how things will turn out, we don't know if anyone will show up, and we fear the consequences or the negative outcomes that we imagine. But often, these fears are based on things that haven't even happened yet. Fear becomes this invisible barrier that blocks us from moving forward.

"So do not fear, for I am with you; do not be dismayed, for I am your God. I will strengthen you and help you; I will uphold you with my righteous right hand." (Isaiah 41:10, NIV)

Fear is one of the main reasons people don't do half of the things they want to do, the things they're supposed to do, or the things they've been called to do. It's that one word: fear. What if we understood that fear is just doing its job, but that most of the time, the fear we feel isn't real? We might feel anxiety or nervousness because we're about to enter into something unknown, but what if we changed our mindset? What if we turned that fear into excitement?

Instead of thinking, "I don't know how this is going to turn out, and it scares me," we could think, "I don't know how this is going to turn out, and I'm excited to find out." Fear is really a negative anticipation of thoughts about something that hasn't even happened. But what if we flipped that script?

QUIET GIRL SZN

DAY 67

Fear does have its place, especially in situations of real danger. If we're in immediate physical danger, fear is there to warn us, to prepare us. But when it comes to starting a new business, trying a new venture, speaking in front of people—are those things dangerous? The answer is probably no. So if it's not dangerous, then the fear you're feeling isn't real. It's just uncertainty about how things will turn out.

What if you approached those situations with excitement instead of fear? What if you said, "I'm excited to see how this turns out, and if it doesn't go as planned, what can I learn from it?" By changing your mindset, you can push past fear. Give fear a different definition and meaning so that it doesn't hold you back. Acknowledge fear for what it is when you're in danger, but otherwise, remove it from your life. Push past it, and move forward to do the things you've been called to do. Just do it.

QUIET TIME

How can you shift your perspective on fear, transforming it from a barrier into a stepping stone for growth and excitement?

PRAYER

Lord, help me to see fear for what it truly is and to push past it when it tries to hold me back. Replace my fear with excitement and confidence, knowing that You are with me every step of the way. In Jesus' name, Amen.

LEAN ALL THE WAY IN!!

Some of the next few days are a little longer because there was more that I wanted to emphasize. I want you to lean all the way into them. I want you to really ponder them and sit with it for it a minute. I want you take time to really reflect on the questions. Because after you are done with this 90 day devotional, I want you to ask yourself one question:

"What will I do different?"

DAY 68

GIRL, ARE YOU FEELING STUCK?

What is at the root of actually feeling stuck? I think when we feel stuck, it's often a result of procrastination driven by a lack of belief—either in ourselves, in the outcome, or in the value of what we want to do. We might not believe that it's going to work, that anyone cares, or that we can even do it. This leads to procrastination, making excuses, and ultimately sabotaging ourselves, leaving us stuck at a certain point with no forward movement.

We get stuck in so many things, especially in fear. When we're stuck, it's almost like a paralyzing feeling, where we don't know what to do next. Sometimes, we're stuck at the last point of failure, internalizing it as if we are the failure, when in reality, it's not you that's a failure.

> "Trust in the Lord with all your heart and lean not on your own understanding; in all your ways submit to him, and he will make your paths straight." (Proverbs 3:5-6, NIV)

Maybe what you were doing just didn't work at that particular moment. Maybe it wasn't the right timing. Maybe something just needed to be tweaked. But you can't allow it to paralyze you to the point where you stay there. If your car broke down on the side of the road, you wouldn't leave it there—you'd figure out whatever needed to be done to get it moving again. Similarly, being stuck is another form of an excuse if we're honest with ourselves. If you're stuck, you need to figure out why you're stuck and where you're stuck.

If you called a tow truck, you couldn't just tell them you're stuck. The first question they'd ask is, "Where are you?" That's where an assessment comes in. Sometimes, we have so much stuff jumbled up in our minds that we haven't identified what's going on. It's like a big treasure box of stuff, and it's all mixed up. You have yet to sort it out. Sometimes, we need to

DAY 68

compartmentalize things, putting them into specific categories so we can know what's what.

When you don't have a system, a plan, or a strategy, it can cause you to feel overwhelmed. When you're overwhelmed, it leaves you in a paralytic mental state, leading to feeling stuck.

So, how do we get unstuck? That's the big question. We get unstuck by sorting through the stuff, figuring out where we're stuck, why we're stuck, and what we need to do to move forward. Change your thinking because sometimes our thoughts are not focused on the right thing. When you feel stuck, take some time to really stop and do a brain dump of everything that's on your mind. Write down all your to-dos, your feelings, and your emotions. Figure out what's bothering you, and let it bother you until you understand why—it's a clue to where you're stuck.

Once you do that, you can start moving into action. You can begin strategizing, planning, setting goals, and moving forward. But first, you have to get yourself unstuck.

QUIET TIME

What areas of your life do you feel stuck in, and how can you take practical steps to identify the root cause and move forward?

PRAYER

Lord, help me to identify the areas where I feel stuck and give me the wisdom and courage to move forward. Help me to trust in You and lean not on my own understanding as I seek clarity and direction. In Jesus' name, Amen.

DAY 69

GIRL, YOU MUST FORGIVE

Forgiveness is a hard pill to swallow. When we are hurting and in pain, it's hard to forgive because we can't get past the emotions of the transgression and the pain it has caused. Forgiveness plays a major role in our lives, determining whether we move forward to do the things we've been called to do or get stuck in unforgiveness. Unforgiveness eats away at the soul, damages relationships, and causes so much pain and turmoil. However, forgiveness is not even about the other person. We have to learn how to reconcile. Reconciliation doesn't necessarily mean mending the relationship, but reconciling to the point where you take ownership of your part, if any, and release the other person from their transgressions because holding onto it only eats away at you.

"Get rid of all bitterness, rage and anger, brawling and slander, along with every form of malice. Be kind and compassionate to one another, forgiving each other, just as in Christ God forgave you." (Ephesians 4:31-32, NIV)

If you have wronged someone or have said or done things that may have offended someone, and forgiveness is needed, grab hold of it and own it. That is where your strength can come from. When you release the things inside of you, you can move forward. Harboring unforgiveness turns into a cancer within your soul, preventing you from being whole; it creeps into many areas of your life. But if you allow healing into your heart, healing becomes the seed of forgiveness. Healing from the hurt because maybe someone didn't even realize that they hurt you, and when they did, maybe they didn't understand the depth of it. Sometimes the person isn't even around anymore to hear, "This is how I'm feeling; this is what was done to me," or "I am so hurt over that."

QUIET GIRL SZN

DAY 69

Unforgiveness keeps us bound and broken. If you don't do many things right in your life, one thing you should always be practicing is learning how to forgive. And if you can practice and learn how to forgive quickly, you will save yourself so much time and so many years of ruined friendships and unanswered prayers. If you are harboring unforgiveness in your heart, release it so that you can be free. If someone has wronged you and has never uttered the words "I'm sorry," "please forgive me," or "I apologize," forgive them anyway.

We walk around with many offenses and emotions, and our souls are scarred. Healing and forgiveness are so important—they are more important than you know. It's not just a matter of holding a grudge; you're literally crushing your soul. Holding onto unforgiveness is like having a clenched fist that you keep squeezing tighter and tighter. But when you release it and open your hand, you get to be free, and not only does it free you, but your forgiveness can also free someone else.

QUIET TIME

Is there someone you need to forgive today, and how can you take steps toward releasing that unforgiveness to find freedom and healing?

PRAYER

Lord, help me to release any unforgiveness that I am holding in my heart. Teach me to forgive as You have forgiven me, so that I can be free and experience the healing that comes from letting go. In Jesus' name, Amen.

DAY 70

GIRL, GREATER IS COMING

Greater is coming, and I know that greater is coming. You have to believe that greater is coming within your heart and truly know it. Out of our mouths, we speak those things that are not as though they are. We get to speak our life into existence. Our life is a series of words followed by actions that lead us to specific places and destinations. If we believe that greater is coming, it means that more is coming, which means we need to prepare ourselves for the more and act accordingly. If you know that you are going to receive a big shipment, you make some room for it. When the shipment comes in, you have somewhere to put it. So if you believe that greater is coming, what do you do?

"Enlarge the place of your tent, stretch your tent curtains wide, do not hold back; lengthen your cords, strengthen your stakes. For you will spread out to the right and to the left; your descendants will dispossess nations and settle in their desolate cities." (Isaiah 54:2-3, NIV)

You act accordingly. You prepare your life for it. You clear the clutter, move things out of the way to prepare for what is coming. It signifies more. If more is coming, more is an increase. If an increase is coming, you have to make room for it. How do you make room for increase? Sometimes it means getting rid of things that no longer serve you to make room for things that do. Just because you used to do things a certain way does not mean that's how you still need to do them. If you believe that greater is coming, you need a mindset shift to prepare for it.

When you know that you are going to receive something, you are open. You can't be closed off to the possibilities of it. If someone is going to put something in your hand and tells you, "Get ready, I'm going to give you this," but you have your hands closed, then you can't receive. They want to give it to you, but you are not open. Outstretched hands are a posture of receiving. When you live in that posture, be open to receive, because that is the only way you will receive. So how will God know you are ready to receive and that greater is coming? Greater is coming, and you get to ask for what you want. Ask for what you want.

QUIET TIME

What steps can you take today to prepare your life, mind, and heart for the greater that is coming? Are you ready to receive?

PRAYER

Lord, help me to prepare for the greater that You have in store for me. Open my heart and mind to receive all that You have planned. Help me to clear the clutter in my life and to trust that greater is coming. In Jesus' name, Amen.

DAY 71

GIRL, IT COULD BE A SET UP

Things are not always going to work out the way we think they should, but things are always working in our favor. Setbacks are going to happen. Life will throw curveballs that derail the process of where we are trying to go and what we are trying to do. But how do you handle it when life gets you off course and makes you start to feel like, "Does this even matter?" Sometimes setbacks can cause people to spiral into depression or have suicidal thoughts because life is not always pretty—but life is purposeful. The very fact that we are here means that there is purpose in our lives.

So often, people run around trying to seek purpose, looking for it as if it's an individual thing, but it's more about finding the purpose in the things you are doing, whatever may be on your heart to do. Sometimes, things are not always going to be as they seem.

> *"And we know that in all things God works for the good of those who love him, who have been called according to his purpose." (Romans 8:28, NIV)*

Sometimes we don't understand what's happening, and life can get so foggy. But it's during those times that there are many lessons to be learned. There is much wisdom to be gleaned from what we consider to be a setback. Sometimes the things we think we want may not even be what's best for us or what we truly need. Setbacks are sometimes just a matter of perspective.

So when you think about a setback, it might mean you need to take a step back and look at the big picture. What part did you play in any of it? Was there something you could have done differently, or maybe it wasn't the right time? When you experience a setback, allow it to give you an opportunity to pause, sit with it for a moment, and allow God to speak to you, minister to you, and show you the things you need to see in the midst of it.

DAY 71

Don't view it as a setback—view it as a moment to pause, long enough to recalibrate and gather your thoughts on what your next moves will be. Maybe it's a time to strategize, figure out what could potentially be, and then thank God for what wasn't. Sometimes we think of what wasn't as a bad thing, but sometimes what wasn't is a good thing because we are constantly being protected from things seen and unseen. So change your perspective on the way you view setbacks, and use them as an opportunity to take a step back. It could be a setup for something greater.

QUIET TIME

How can you change your perspective on setbacks to see them as opportunities for growth, recalibration, and deeper understanding of God's plan for your life?

PRAYER

Lord, help me to see setbacks not as defeats but as opportunities to pause, reflect, and recalibrate. Give me the wisdom to understand the lessons You are teaching me and the courage to trust in Your purpose for my life. In Jesus' name, Amen.

DAY 72

GIRL, DON'T WORRY

Obstacles are always going to be there, but you can't allow them to stop you. If we wait for the perfect moment when everything is lined up before we do anything, we'll never accomplish anything. It's about how we maneuver and navigate through the obstacles, how we deal with challenges, and how we take care of what needs to be done so we can move forward. Sometimes, we see things as obstacles when they are simply the inevitable troubles of life. God told us we would have troubles, but we don't have to be discouraged by them. We can take heart because He has overcome the world and all the challenges in our lives. There is nothing that has happened to us or will happen that we can't grow past.

Will it be painful? Definitely. Will we need to heal? Absolutely. But obstacles should not stop us from moving forward. They may come in the form of roadblocks that delay us from reaching a specific destination, but they should not stop us. Even if we need to reframe momentarily, regroup, reassess, renew, or reinvent ourselves, we should do so without allowing obstacles to stop us. Take care of what needs to be done and then get back to whatever it is that you have been called to do.

"I have told you these things, so that in me you may have peace. In this world you will have trouble. But take heart! I have overcome the world." (John 16:33, NIV)

How do you overcome obstacles? You do just that—you overcome them. You go around them, under them, or over them. You do what you can. Pray about it, seek wisdom, seek wise counsel, and allow God to work it out in your life. Sometimes, we place too much emphasis on the obstacle itself, rather than creating a system to deal with it.

DAY 72

Having a system in place means that when obstacles arise, there are basic questions and steps you can follow to troubleshoot and navigate your way through them. For example, when something happens and it appears to be a roadblock, a challenge, or an obstacle, ask yourself, "What can I do in this moment?" If there's something you can do, then do it. If there's nothing you can do, then pray about it. Allow God to give you the wisdom to know how to move, what to do, and who to call. It's through prayer that things are revealed, and in those quiet, still moments, you can hear that still, small voice guiding and directing you down the paths you need to take. So how do you overcome obstacles? You just do.

QUIET TIME

What obstacles are you facing right now, and how can you shift your focus from the obstacle itself to creating a system for overcoming it with God's guidance?

PRAYER

Lord, help me to see obstacles as opportunities to grow and learn. Give me the wisdom and strength to navigate through them and the faith to trust that You are guiding me every step of the way. In Jesus' name, Amen.

DAY 73

GIRL, THIS HAS TO STOP

Procrastination; this is a big one. The avoidance of it all. Why do we procrastinate? Overwhelm sometimes leads us to procrastinate because we don't always know where to start. We sometimes feel like it's too much, or at the root of it, we probably doubt that it could even work. We allow fear to step in and cloud our judgment, making us think it's not going to work. So we procrastinate, and with our procrastination, what we're actually doing is delaying what we consider to be the inevitable failure. If we continue to procrastinate, which means we never move forward to actually do the thing, then we never reach a point of failure. And failure makes us feel like we've failed, as opposed to realizing that what we did just didn't work. So we secretly sabotage ourselves, but that's a discussion for another day.

"A sluggard's appetite is never filled, but the desires of the diligent are fully satisfied." (Proverbs 13:4, NIV)

Procrastination comes in, and we keep putting things off. "Oh, I'll take care of that tomorrow. I'll do that tomorrow," but tomorrow never comes because all we are left with every single day is today. Tomorrow never comes, and procrastination has to be killed at the root. We really have to dig to the root of why we procrastinate, which often ties back to the fear that something will fail. And because we don't move forward, even if what we set out to do doesn't work, we never discover that it's just a method that didn't work, not an indication of who we are.

Procrastination also has the ability to make you feel like you are a failure. That's why so much emotion is attached to it—because you're not doing what you know you're supposed to do. By holding back, you think you're protecting yourself, but you're actually hurting yourself because you never get to the point where you feel accomplished or finished with

DAY 73

something. If you continually live a life of procrastination, you're setting yourself up for failure.

If you're going to go through the process, go through it. If you're going to fail, fail quickly. And don't look at it as a failure; look at it as a lesson. When you take the word "failure" out and replace it with, "What lesson am I trying to learn from this?" or "What lesson can I take from this to apply to the next steps?" it changes the outcome of what you're doing. You don't have to be afraid of the unknown. And that's what procrastination is really rooted in—it's the fear of the unknown.

So how do we cure procrastination? We do the thing, even though it makes us uncomfortable, and get it over with; otherwise, it's just going to keep weighing on your mind. Procrastination is heavy—it really is because you carry it with you every single day. But what if you just released it? What if you released the thing you know you're supposed to do so that you can walk into the season of life that you know you're supposed to walk into? You know it in your heart, and procrastination is just the fear stopping you—it's gripping you and robbing you. Allow procrastination to steal no more.

QUIET TIME

What is one thing you've been procrastinating on, and how can you take the first step today to move forward and release the fear that's holding you back?

PRAYER

Lord, help me to overcome the fear that leads to procrastination. Give me the courage to take the first step, to move forward, and to trust in Your guidance as I walk into the season You have prepared for me. In Jesus' name, Amen.

DAY 74

GIRL, YOUR PAIN WASN'T FOR NOTHING

When we are going through things, we can't always see the purpose in the pain.

How could something so tragic, something so horrible, be purposeful? God said that He can use anything. He may not have caused it, but He can use it. He said that all things work together for good. If all things work together for good for those who are called according to His purpose and His plan, and if He knew us when He created us—meaning He had a plan for us—then it's not just going to work out for some people; it can work out for everyone if we allow it to.

> *"Praise be to the God and Father of our Lord Jesus Christ, the Father of compassion and the God of all comfort, who comforts us in all our troubles, so that we can comfort those in any trouble, with the comfort we ourselves receive from God."*
> *(2 Corinthians 1:3-4, NIV)*

Sometimes we go through pain and get stuck in it. We get stuck at the point of our last pain, and it paralyzes us. We are not able to move because we can't understand why—we get stuck in the "why" instead of focusing on the purpose that can be fulfilled through the healing of it. You can't even move to the essence of the purpose of pain without first understanding that there is healing in it. Healing is where the purpose comes in. It's not pain, then purpose; it's pain, healing, then purpose.

Through healing, you begin to mend, to love, and to forgive. It's a process with stages that you go through before the purpose is materialized enough to be tangible and used. How can someone who has been homeless, sexually abused, and violated by someone

DAY 74

who was supposed to love, honor, and protect her—a high school dropout with a host of issues—use all that pain for purpose? It's through the healing process.

When you begin to heal and pray, asking God to show you how to remove the remnants of the pain and recycle your life to help others, you start to see how your pain can turn into purpose. While going through so much pain may cause us to be inwardly focused—rightfully so, because that's where the healing takes place—once you go through that process, you can see others who may have experienced similar pains. At that point, you can turn your pain into purpose and help someone else.

Often, we don't realize that the things we've gone through were not necessarily for us. Maybe you are the conduit through which God can flow to be an answer to somebody else's question or a solution to somebody's problem, but only because you went through it. There is purpose in your pain.

QUIET TIME

What pain have you experienced that could be used to help others, and how can you begin the healing process to discover the purpose in that pain?

PRAYER

Lord, help me to see the purpose in my pain. Guide me through the healing process so that I can use my experiences to help others and glorify Your name. In Jesus' name, Amen.

DAY 75

GIRL, STOP BEING ALL OVER THE PLACE

In order to achieve goals, you need to be disciplined enough to stick with them. Achieving goals requires creating a process and implementing systems to track your progress, determine if you are on track, and meet deadlines. They say that goals without a plan are just dreams. To not only create but also achieve a goal, you must intentionally take steps toward it. The first step is actually quite simple: writing it down. Sometimes we neglect these basic actions. For example, In the bible, Naaman was told by the prophet Elisha to dip in the Jordan River seven times. Although the Jordan River wasn't the cleanest, it was a simple task. Naaman was upset because he expected something more elaborate. Sometimes, we fail to reach our goals because we make them out to be more complicated than they need to be.

> *"The plans of the diligent lead to profit as surely as haste leads to poverty." (Proverbs 21:5, NIV)*

It's really simple. You write the goal down, then you write what the end result should be and the completion date. Next, you start working backward to determine what steps you need to take to get from point A to point Z. If you write out the steps in between, and then start completing them, before you know it, you will have achieved your goal. Sometimes we can't achieve goals because we're all over the place, and this is where discipline comes in.

Discipline is needed to stick to whatever you say that you're going to do. Be disciplined enough to say, whether it's one thing a day, two things a day, or whatever it is that you commit to. Discipline is a regimented routine that allows you to stick to a specific behavior and pattern. That's what you need to do. So if you are looking to achieve goals, writing them down is the first step. Staying committed and disciplined is the next step. These are actually small steps that make a big difference.

QUIET TIME

What goals have you set that require more discipline, and how can you begin implementing small, consistent steps to achieve them?

PRAYER

Lord, grant me the discipline and commitment to follow through on the goals You have placed in my heart. Help me to stay focused and take intentional steps toward the fulfillment of these goals. In Jesus' name, Amen.

DAY 76

GIRL, YOU GOT THIS

So many times, we sabotage ourselves, unbeknownst to us, not realizing that this is exactly what we are doing.

We make excuses and procrastinate, all because we don't believe that we are good enough. When things happen that are good for us, we find a way to sabotage them. When we don't do things that we are supposed to do, knowing in our hearts that this is what we have been called to do, what we belong to do, and what we want to do, we sabotage ourselves because we don't feel worthy. We don't feel like it could happen to us, or we don't believe that it is happening for us. So we secretly find a way to not make it work, so that we don't have to be accountable for it, or so that we can say, "See, at least I tried," but that's not it.

When you sabotage yourself, what you're doing is working against yourself. Think about sabotaging. If someone were sabotaging someone else, what would they do? Then think about the ways that you do that to yourself. How you don't set yourself up for success because you don't believe that it's true.

> *"I can do all this through him who gives me strength."*
> *(Philippians 4:13, NIV)*

So you walk in a manner and in a way that doesn't lead you in the direction of what you want or where you want to go. Secretly not believing and doing little minuscule things that rob you of things that you need in your life—sabotaging yourself is a real thing. Stop sabotaging yourself. Stop doing that to yourself. If it's in your heart, believe that you can do it. Ask God to give you wisdom. Ask God to give you instructions on how to move forward.

DAY 76

We have to stop sabotaging ourselves. Stop worrying about what other people are doing and comparing yourself to them. Look at the life that you have been called to live, and then do your best to live that life with excellence. If there's something that you know that you have been called to do and it's been on your heart, do everything within your power to do it. Ask God for wisdom, strategy, and insight. Ask God for favor so that you can succeed, because that's what we want—to succeed at the things we have been called to do.

Knowing that success looks different for everyone, you don't have to worry about what success looks like for someone else. What does success look like for you? Lean into that, plan, and pray for the best. Do all that you know how to do without making excuses or procrastinating. Think of ways to improve yourself. Think good thoughts. Be good to people. Say good things out of your mouth. Move in a good, great, and excellent way.

QUIET TIME

What areas in your life are you sabotaging yourself, and how can you begin to trust God's plan and move forward without fear?

PRAYER

Lord, help me to recognize when I am sabotaging myself and give me the strength to overcome fear and doubt. Guide me to walk in faith, trusting that I am worthy of the plans You have for me. In Jesus' name, Amen.

DAY 77

GIRL, SHARE YOUR STORY

We have all gone through a journey in life, and someone is going through the same journey you've gone through and have come out of. You could potentially help them to know that while they're going through it and experiencing such trouble and turmoil, there is light at the end of the tunnel. When you share your story, it gives hope to people that, no matter what, they can come through it. Sometimes, when we're in it, we can't see the light, and it seems like all hope has been lost. In those dark moments, that's when people need to hear it the most.

"They triumphed over him by the blood of the Lamb and by the word of their testimony; they did not love their lives so much as to shrink from death." (Revelation 12:11, NIV)

There are so many people who have been in such dark moments that they have committed suicide, tried to commit suicide, or fallen into deep depression because they think that in that moment, this is it, and they can't see a way out. When we share our story and someone is able to resonate with it and hear that you were there but now you're here, and if you can share with them the steps you've taken to come out of it, that can help shine some light on how they can potentially get out of it.

But if you keep your mouth closed and never say a word, and never share any of the struggles you've gone through and how you've overcome them, how can you be of service to anyone else? That means you think your entire life is self-serving and only for you, and it's not. When we understand that we are all here to serve one another, to glean and learn from each other, and to travel this road called life together, we would see such a difference in how we go through things. We would be able to help and support one another on this journey.

DAY 77

That's why it's so important that someone hears your story. We are overcome by our testimony. Someone is able to overcome the situations they are in because of another's testimony. Share your testimony. Your testimony is a living testament to what you've gone through and have come out of. The fact that you're still standing, still here, and still have life, health, and breath in your body means somebody needs to hear your story. Somebody needs to hear what you've gone through so they too can have hope.

QUIET TIME

What part of your life story can you share today that might bring hope and encouragement to someone else?

PRAYER

Lord, give me the courage to share my testimony with others. Help me to see how my story can be a source of hope and strength for someone else who may be going through a difficult time. In Jesus' name, Amen.

DAY **78**

GIRL, STOP SETTLING

Stop settling. You don't have to settle, suffer, or stay stuck. Set yourself free. When I think about settling, I imagine that we reach a point where we feel like this is all that life has to offer us. It feels like we're stuck, unsure of where to go or what to do next. But maybe it's more than just being stuck—it's often rooted in fear. Fear of failure, fear of not knowing how to do something, fear of what others might think, or fear of not having enough resources to start. All these fears work together to keep us in the same place, longing to move forward but unable to take that first step.

> *"See, I am doing a new thing! Now it springs up; do you not perceive it? I am making a way in the wilderness and streams in the wasteland." Isaiah 43:19 (NIV)*

When fear holds you back, you settle in a place that is beneath your potential. You stay where you are, even while longing to be somewhere else. But what if you just moved forward with what you know, trusting God with the rest? Either it will work, or you will learn a valuable lesson. Either way, it will ultimately work for your good. Don't let fear keep you stuck. Life is passing you by every single day, and you are wasting time when you stay stuck.

Think about it like a car stuck on the side of the road. It can't move because something is wrong—maybe the battery is dead or the starter is broken. The car can't stay there, so a tow truck comes, takes it to the shop, does a diagnostic, and identifies the problem so it can be fixed. After it's fixed, the car can get back on the road. What if you did the same thing with your life? What if you took a moment to do a diagnostic and asked yourself, "Why am I stuck? What am I afraid of? What

DAY 78

do I want to do? Why do I want to do it? How do I need to get there?"

Once you figure out why you're stuck, you can take steps to fix it and move forward. Don't settle for being stuck when God has so much more in store for you. Take yourself through this process, seek God's guidance, and set yourself free to move into the purposes and plans He has for your life.

QUIET TIME

What area of your life are you settling in, and how can you take a step today to move past the fear that's holding you back?

PRAYER

Lord, help me to stop settling for less than what You've called me to. Show me the areas where I'm stuck and help me overcome the fears that are holding me back. Give me the courage to move forward in faith, trusting that You are guiding my steps and that everything will work together for my good. In Jesus' name, Amen.

DAY 79

GIRL, YOU ARE WORTHY

Struggling with insecurities is a real thing. We often become insecure about many different things, and mostly, it's due to what has happened to us in our childhood. Our insecurities become ingrained within us because we may not have been validated or esteemed when we were younger for many different reasons. When we are told that we aren't good enough or made to feel like we don't matter, it affects how we show up in the world, how we feel about ourselves, and the beliefs we hold about ourselves. These insecurities ultimately hold us back from being the best we can be and from living the life that God has called us to live because we don't believe it.

"I praise you because I am fearfully and wonderfully made; your works are wonderful, I know that full well."
(Psalm 139:14, NIV)

We can be insecure about so many things—our weight, our hair, how we look, how we sound, what we don't have, whether it's education, our demographics, or where we live. The struggles with these insecurities really stop us from moving forward. To overcome these issues, we need to examine our lives and address the things that plague us. We need to dig into the root of why we feel this way, understand what it's rooted in, and determine what we can change about it. We should focus on feeling our best and moving in the direction we want to go.

We all struggle with different things, but we all matter. We all look, talk, and walk differently, but that does not diminish our worth. We don't have to compare ourselves to one another. If we just stand by the promises of what we have been called to do and move in that direction, we don't have to get caught up in being insecure about anything. We can be securely confident in the fact that God created us, knows us, and has a plan for our lives. No more struggling with insecurities—stand securely and confidently in the truth of who God created you to be.

QUIET TIME

What insecurities are holding you back from fully embracing the person God created you to be, and how can you begin to address them with His help?

PRAYER

Lord, help me to see myself through Your eyes. Give me the strength to overcome my insecurities and to stand confidently in the truth of who You have created me to be. In Jesus' name, Amen.

DAY 80

GIRL, CHANGE YOUR MIND

Transformational thinking means changing your mindset so you can think differently about life and the things you are called to do. Transformational thinking is not thinking how you used to think. It's a change in the process so that you can move forward. If we don't change the way we think, we will never change the way we live. Our thought process and our words guide our actions, and we need to change our lives so that we can be better, do better, achieve more, and move forward in the purposes and plans that God has for us. But if we get stuck in our old way of thinking and do things the old way, we won't be able to move forward. The person you are is different from the person you are going to be. There needs to be a shift, so you can't be who you are and who you want to be at the same time. There has to be some forward thinking and movement.

> "Do not conform to the pattern of this world, but be transformed by the renewing of your mind. Then you will be able to test and approve what God's will is—his good, pleasing and perfect will." (Romans 12:2, NIV)

If you want to get to a specific place or achieve a specific thing, you need to figure out what is required to stand in that place or achieve that goal. What do you need to do, have, or become? Then, determine the steps needed to transform your life to reach those goals. You won't be able to get there without a transformation, which starts with changing your thought process. If you have to do something different, don't negate small changes. Transformation happens in increments, and these small steps will move you forward in the right direction. If you stay still, that's where you will always be.

DAY 80

You have to be able to put one foot in front of the other. You need to step forward and take the necessary steps required to do the things you have been called to do. Be transformed by the renewing of your mind. So how do you transform your life? You renew your mind. How do you renew your mind? You adopt a different way of thinking. You introduce different inputs: you read different books, go to different places, and speak with different people. You bring new information into your life to create change. If you keep putting the same old things in, you'll get the same results.

If you want something different, you need to do something different. You must change your thought process to change the way you live. On the journey to transforming your thoughts, you will receive epiphanies, "wow" moments, and innovative ideas. As you start moving forward with them, you'll see your life change before your eyes. Before you know it, you begin to live a life that is barely recognizable because you decided to change something. This is where people often get stuck. You wonder why your life still looks the same and why it hasn't changed. It's because you haven't changed your thought process regarding how you live or what you want to do. Change your thinking, and it will inevitably change your living.

QUIET TIME

What is one area of your life where you need to change your thinking in order to see transformation? How can you begin to renew your mind in this area?

PRAYER

Lord, help me to renew my mind and adopt a new way of thinking that aligns with Your will for my life. Guide me in making the changes I need to move forward and live out the purpose You have for me. In Jesus' name, Amen.

DAY 81

GIRL, JUST TRUST GOD

What are we trusting in? When I think about trust, I think about stepping out on faith because it's not an easy thing to do. Being able to say, "Okay, God, I trust you in this process," and not have doubt in the midst of it is challenging. How do we do that? Because doubt always creeps up. Doubt is at the center of the unknown, and sometimes we doubt because maybe we don't believe that we could, so doubt and our belief system kind of go hand in hand with what it is that we believe. So when I think about doubt, I think doubt is us not trusting ourselves to know if we could do it or if we should do it, or heck, we just don't know. And so doubt creeps in. But then on the flip side of doubt, there needs to be this trust and this knowing that going into it says, "Yeah, I don't really know how it's gonna be, but I am going to trust that no matter what, it will work out good."

"When I am afraid, I put my trust in you. In God, whose word I praise—in God I trust and am not afraid. What can mere mortals do to me?" Psalm 56:3-4 (NIV)

If we live in doubt, then we're not able to really move forward. And if we do move forward, it's not with confidence. So whatever it is that we do, we want to be able to move forward with the confidence of knowing that no matter what, it's all going to work out. Even if it doesn't work out the way that we thought it should, at least you tried it. Living in doubt also leads to living with regrets because when you doubt certain things, a lot of times it stops you from moving forward.

DAY 81

Doubt is the opposite of trust, and in doubt, sometimes it's more about saying, "You know, I'm not really sure how this is going to be," and that's okay as long as it doesn't stop you. If it stops you at "I'm not sure how this is going to be, so I'm not going to do it," then that's not a good thing. Trust the process and trust in the journey to allow it to lead you to places that you probably would've never, ever gone or never even experienced had you not taken that step of faith.

So the whole thing is to be able to just move and not allow doubt or fear to hold you back. Trust that it will all work out even if it's not the way that you think, the way that it should, or even the way that it could, all because you were able to step out there and try it. So trust yourself enough to know, to say, "Okay, I am going to do this," and don't doubt that it'll work because you never know what it could be. And don't allow doubt to stop you in your tracks from moving forward with what you've been called to do.

QUIET TIME

What areas of your life are you struggling to trust God in, and how can you begin to replace doubt with faith?

PRAYER

Lord, help me to trust You fully and not be paralyzed by doubt. Give me the courage to step out in faith, knowing that You are guiding my steps and that everything will work together for my good. In Jesus' name, Amen.

DAY 82

GIRL, WHAT ARE YOU PASSIONATE ABOUT

What does it mean to unlock your passion? Unlocking your passion is like going on a journey of self-discovery. It's about uncovering the things that truly ignite your soul by exploring and trying new experiences. I remember how much I used to talk about finding your passion and purpose, but I've come to realize that unlocking your passion is an even deeper process. It's not just about finding what you like; it's about discovering what you love so deeply that it brings you profound joy and fulfillment.

When you unlock your passion, it goes beyond mere enjoyment. It taps into something that gives you a deep sense of satisfaction and purpose. There's no greater feeling than when you unlock that passion and find yourself doing something that aligns perfectly with what you were meant to do.

> *"Take delight in the Lord, and he will give you the desires of your heart."*
> (Psalm 37:4, NIV)

Discovering your passion often involves stepping out of your comfort zone, trying new things, and being open to where these experiences might lead you. Sometimes, we don't find our passion because we haven't tried enough or because we've allowed fear to keep us from exploring new possibilities. It's okay to try different things because that's how you figure out what you enjoy and what truly resonates with you.

QUIET GIRL SZN

DAY **82**

Unlocking your passion means recognizing that it may be hidden or dormant within you, waiting to be discovered. It's a process of digging deep, experimenting, and leaning into those activities or pursuits that make you feel alive. Passion doesn't just appear; it's something you uncover over time through the journey of life. As you explore and embrace new experiences, you'll gradually discover that one thing—or maybe even several things—that truly makes your heart sing. And that's the essence of unlocking your passion.

QUIET TIME

What new experiences or interests have you been avoiding that could potentially unlock a hidden passion in your life?

PRAYER

Lord, help me to explore new opportunities with an open heart and mind. Guide me to discover the passions You have placed within me and give me the courage to pursue them with joy and determination. In Jesus' name, Amen.

DAY 83

GIRL, WHAT'S EATING YOU?

What's Eating You? There is a connection between emotional wealth and physical health.

Sometimes, we turn to food not just for nourishment but to comfort ourselves emotionally. It's easy to get caught up in eating to soothe our feelings, without realizing the toll it takes on our physical bodies. We might think we're satisfying a need, but in reality, we're not addressing the root cause. Often, we eat when we're not even hungry—perhaps because we're procrastinating, feeling tired, or simply out of habit. Food becomes our go-to solution, whether we're sad, stressed, or even celebrating.

> "Do you not know that your bodies are temples of the Holy Spirit, who is in you, whom you have received from God? You are not your own; you were bought at a price. Therefore honor God with your bodies."
> (1 Corinthians 6:19-20, NIV)

We need to learn how to disconnect our emotions from our eating habits. This isn't easy, especially when food has become intertwined with our emotional responses. But it's crucial. We have to explore why we overeat and take a hard look at our emotional health. The truth is, emotional health and physical health are deeply connected. When one is out of balance, the other often follows.

So, what's really eating you? Or rather, what are you eating to combat what's eating you emotionally? Many of us use food to fill an emotional void, seeking comfort in unhealthy ways. This is why we turn to comfort food, but have you noticed how certain foods make you feel tired or sluggish? We need to reconsider how we use food and think about the long-term impact on our lives and health.

DAY 83

Often, the issues that drive us to overeat are the same ones we avoid addressing. Whether it's unresolved pain, unforgiveness, or deep-seated fears, these emotions gnaw at us from the inside. The key to overcoming them isn't in the food we eat but in dealing with the root causes. This might mean having difficult conversations, whether with others or ourselves. And sometimes, we need help—seeking a therapist or a counselor can be a powerful step toward emotional healing.

What's eating you doesn't have to control your life. You can take charge of your emotional and physical well-being, starting with small, manageable changes. It's not about drastic transformations overnight but about incremental changes that lead to long-term improvement. Even small steps, like reading a page of something that nourishes your mind, can set you on a path to a healthier, more fulfilling life.

If you want different results, you need to do something different. Start with small, intentional steps. Over time, these small changes will add up, leading to significant improvements in your emotional and physical health. Remember, your emotional health can lead to emotional wealth—the fullness and richness of life that you truly desire.

QUIET TIME

What are the emotional triggers that cause you to turn to food for comfort, and how can you start addressing them in a healthier way?

PRAYER

Lord, help me to identify and address the emotional needs that drive me to unhealthy habits. Give me the strength to seek healing and to treat my body as the temple You created it to be. Guide me in making small, positive changes that lead to a fuller, healthier life. In Jesus' name, Amen.

DAY 84

GIRL, YOU MAY NEED TO WALK AWAY

Walking Away Takes Courage and is never easy. It's a decision that comes after many moments of reflection, hesitation, and often, pain. It's not just about physically leaving something behind—whether it's a place, a person, or even a situation. Walking away also means releasing the emotional and mental hold those things may have over you. The hardest part? The uncertainty of what lies ahead. The comfort of the familiar keeps us tethered to situations long past their expiration date. Even when we know deep down that something isn't right, the fear of the unknown often holds us back.

"Have I not commanded you? Be strong and courageous. Do not be afraid; do not be discouraged, for the Lord your God will be with you wherever you go."

Joshua 1:9 (NIV)

Looking back, the signs were always there—the warnings, the red flags, the moments when you felt uneasy or unsettled. But it's easy to ignore those signs when we're clinging to what feels safe, even if it's no longer serving us. Then, one day, you find yourself at rock bottom, feeling trapped and uncertain, wondering how you got there.

At that moment, you have a choice: stay in the ditch or muster the courage to climb out. Both choices require bravery. Staying takes courage because it means you're willing to face the discomfort of what's holding you down. Leaving takes courage because it means stepping into an unknown future. The key is to ask God for guidance and wisdom. During those moments when you come to that fork in the road, present your dilemma to God. Trust that He will lead you in the right direction.

QUIET TIME

What has God been showing you that it's time to walk away from, and how can you trust Him to guide your next steps?

PRAYER

Lord, help me to recognize the signs when it's time to walk away from things that no longer serve Your purpose in my life. Give me the courage to step into the unknown, trusting that You will guide and protect me. Lead me in Your wisdom, and make my path straight as I submit my decisions to You. In Jesus' name, Amen.

DAY 85

GIRL, YOU ARE GOING TO BE ALRIGHT

Hold On! This Too Shall Pass. I know right now it doesn't seem like it. It doesn't feel like it. When you're going through difficult times, the pain can feel overwhelming. It's easy to get lost in the darkness, unable to see a way out or even believe that there's light on the other side. But in these moments, pause and remember—look back over your life and see where God's hand has been faithful. Reflect on the times He brought you through, and hold onto that. Find something, anything, that anchors you when everything else seems shaky.

"God is our refuge and strength, an ever-present help in trouble." Psalm 46:1 (NIV)

Ask God to be your rock, your safe place when the storm feels unbearable. Although it may not feel like it now, remember that this, too, shall pass. Lean on your community—reach out to friends who will not just listen but who will also pray for you. Even if they don't know the specifics, they can lift you up in prayer and stand in the gap when you feel too weary.

Continue to seek God. Tell Him everything; your fears, your doubts, your worries. Don't hold back because what concerns you also concerns Him. He cares deeply for you and has promised never to leave you, even in the darkest moments. Trust that He will heal your heart and lead you through this season.

QUIET TIME

In moments of struggle, can you recall a time when God has brought you through before? How can you trust Him to do it again?

PRAYER

Lord, I come to You in this difficult time, feeling overwhelmed and unsure of what to do. Please be my refuge and strength. Help me to see Your hand in my life, even when it feels so dark. Heal my heart, calm my fears, and remind me that You are always with me, no matter the storm. In Jesus' name, Amen.

DAY 86

GIRL, DON'T RUN AHEAD OF GOD

God's timing is perfect. I remember when I used to ask Him, "When is it going to be my turn?" I would see others around me seemingly winning, getting ahead, and moving forward, while I felt like I was stuck on the sidelines. It's easy to get caught up in comparing your journey to someone else's, thinking that they're going further, faster, but we don't always see the full picture.

God's timing is perfect. Sometimes a "no" is actually a blessing, because what we think we want isn't always what's best for us. We can only see a small part, but God sees everything—the past, the present, and the future. A "wait" could mean that the situation isn't ready, or maybe you're not ready yet. If we trust in God's timing, we can rest knowing that when it does happen, it will be the right time. It will be perfect, and it will unfold exactly as it was meant to.

> "There is a time for everything, and a season for every activity under the heavens." Ecclesiastes 3:1 (NIV)

I can think of countless times when I asked God for something or wished to be in a certain place, only to later discover that His "no" or "wait" was for my own good. I'm so thankful for His hand of protection, guiding me and shielding me from things I didn't realize I needed protection from. Trust that God knows the bigger picture, and He is always working in your favor.

Instead of rushing ahead of Him, trust His timing. Walk in the way He is leading you, and you will always be where you are supposed to be, with what you are supposed to have, at just the right moment.

QUIET TIME

Can you think of a time when God's timing proved to be perfect, even though you couldn't see it in the moment?

PRAYER

Lord, help me to trust Your perfect timing. Even when I feel impatient or unsure, I know that You see the bigger picture and are working all things together for my good. Give me peace in the waiting and wisdom to walk in step with You. Thank You for Your protection, guidance, and love. In Jesus' name, Amen.

DAY 87

GIRL, HOLD ON

Sometimes things are going to be hard. There will be moments when you're faced with tough choices and difficult decisions. Life won't always look the way you expect, and outcomes may not unfold the way you imagine. But even in those times, trust that God is working, even when you can't see the way ahead. Sometimes, you have to let go of how you think things should turn out and rest in knowing that God is working things out for your good.

> *"And we know that in all things God works for the good of those who love him, who have been called according to his purpose."*
> Romans 8:28 (NIV)

Right now, it may not feel good. You might not see how any good could possibly come from what you're going through. But on the other side of this hardship, there is breakthrough waiting. The sun will shine again, and things will get better. Holding on and persevering through the process and enduring the difficulties will strengthen you, sustain you, and keep you grounded.

In those moments when life feels overwhelming, it's important to remember that God's timing is different from ours. His perspective is eternal, while ours is often clouded by the here and now. We may not understand why things are happening the way they are, but we can trust in God's love and His promise to work all things together for our good. Each trial or hardship has the potential to develop character, patience, and a deeper relationship with God, refining us for the future He has planned.

QUIET TIME

What difficult situation can you surrender to God, trusting that He is working it out for your good?

PRAYER

Lord, in the hard times, remind me to trust You. Help me to surrender my expectations and hold onto Your promise that all things are working for my good. When I can't see the way, help me to trust that You are guiding me. Thank You for being my rock and steadying me through the storms of life. In Jesus' name, Amen.

DAY 88

GIRL, BE QUIET

There's so much to be said about the quiet times and the quiet seasons of life—the moments of reflection, calm, and stillness. It's interesting how the quiet can sometimes seem so loud, without a sound being made, and yet, it's in those moments when you hear the most.

Have you ever tried listening and talking at the same time? It's impossible because your focus is divided. In those still and quiet moments, allow God time to speak to you. Often, we say our prayers, share our worries, and tell God all about our cares. He is concerned and He wants to know. But after we pour out our hearts, we get up and move on without giving God time to respond.

> *"After the earthquake came a fire, but the Lord was not in the fire. And after the fire came a gentle whisper." 1 Kings 19:12 (NIV)*

In those moments of silence, simply say, "Speak, Lord, your servant is listening." God speaks in various ways—through people, circumstances, and even the subtle signs around you. When you position your heart to listen, you begin to notice those divine whispers that guide you.

Reflection and assessment should become a regular part of your daily life. This practice can make this season of your life different; a season of shifting, purpose, and divine movement. When you're in tune with God, He can reveal hidden things, things you couldn't see before. Remember, No eye has seen, and no ear has heard, what He has in store for you.

QUIET GIRL SZN

QUIET TIME

How can you cultivate stillness and silence in your life to better hear from God?

PRAYER

Lord, teach me to embrace the quiet moments in my life. Help me to be still and wait for Your voice. When I pour out my heart to You, give me the patience to listen for Your response. Reveal the hidden things I need to see, and guide me in this season of reflection and purpose. In Jesus' name, Amen.

DAY 89

GIRL, IT'S YOUR RESPONSIBILITY

You are responsible for your joy. Recently, I experienced a situation that left me feeling upset and disconnected from someone important to me. I found myself spending a few days away from home because I was frustrated and couldn't understand why the other person didn't see things from my perspective. I was deep in my feelings, unsure of where things were headed or how we would move forward.

During my time away, I still didn't gain full clarity, but it gave me the opportunity to sit with myself and reflect. When I came back home, something had shifted within me. God showed me a different perspective. Even though nothing physically changed in the situation, there was a change in my mindset.

"Rejoice in the Lord always. I will say it again: Rejoice!"
Philippians 4:4 (NIV)

In that moment, God revealed to me that no one else is responsible for my peace, my joy, or my happiness. Those things are up to me. By expecting someone else to carry the weight of my emotional well-being, I was giving them too much power over my life. This shift in my thinking allowed me to view the other person differently. I no longer saw them as responsible for my fulfillment, and it released me from an unhealthy expectation.

You are responsible for your joy. You are responsible for your peace. You are responsible for your happiness. No one else can or should carry that burden for you. When you take ownership of your emotional well-being, you step into a freedom that allows you to thrive, regardless of external circumstances.

QUIET TIME

Are you placing responsibility for your happiness and joy on someone else? How can you reclaim that responsibility today?

PRAYER

Lord, thank You for reminding me that my joy, peace, and happiness come from You and are my responsibility to nurture. Help me to stop expecting others to fulfill what only You can provide. Teach me to rejoice in all circumstances and to seek Your peace above all else. In Jesus' name, Amen.

DAY 90

GIRL, LET'S CELEBRATE

YAYYYYYYYYYY! You've reached 90 days. They may not have been 90 consecutive days, but you've made it to this 90th devotional, and that's worth celebrating! Take a moment to recognize the consistency, dedication, and perseverance it took to sit down, commit, and complete this journey. Because that's exactly what I'm going to do—celebrate the journey and reflect on all the steps that got me here.

Writing this 90-day devotional has been an emotional rollercoaster filled with challenges, moments of doubt, and uncertainty. Every devotional I've shared came from personal experiences—things I've walked through, lessons I've learned, and revelations that God placed on my heart. I've combed through my journals, carefully selecting the topics that have resonated with me and, I pray, with you. And while it wasn't easy, I stayed the course. You stayed the course. We did it!

> "Brothers and sisters, I do not consider myself yet to have taken hold of it. But one thing I do: Forgetting what is behind and straining toward what is ahead, I press on toward the goal to win the prize for which God has called me heavenward in Christ Jesus."
> Philippians 3:13-14 (NIV)

There were moments when I felt like quitting. There were days when I questioned whether I could finish this project. But every time I read through the devotionals, as I wrote and reflected, they sank deeper into my soul, reminding me of who I am, who God created me to be, and what He has called me to do. I hope they did the same for you.

So, my question for you is: now what? The devotional may have come to an end, but your journey is far from over. What are you going to do differently moving forward? How will you allow God to use you for His glory in the days ahead? I know the devotional is complete, but there are still questions to be answered, steps to be taken, and a purpose to be fulfilled.

QUIET TIME

Now that you've completed this devotional journey, what is your next step? How will you continue to seek God's purpose for your life?

PRAYER

Lord, thank You for this journey. Thank You for the growth, the challenges, and the revelations. Help me to continue seeking Your purpose in my life, to press forward with faith, and to walk boldly in the calling you have for me. May this journey be just the beginning of even greater things. In Jesus' name, Amen.

About the Author, Towanda McEachern

Towanda McEachern is a transformational life coach, author, and speaker on a mission to help women heal, transform, and reclaim their lives. After facing her own struggles with identity and purpose, she embarked on a journey of self-discovery that led her to empower others to do the same. Through her business, **A Life Recycled®**, Towanda has created workshops and retreats designed to guide women through healing, self-discovery, and personal growth.

Her passion for helping others began with her own desire to be a role model for her daughters. Through quiet time, prayer, and reflection, she found her true calling—to lead other women out of emotional turmoil and into a place of wholeness and empowerment. Towanda's unique blend of practical, therapeutic guidance and spiritual insight has helped countless women unlock their potential and walk confidently in their God-given purpose.

In 2022, Towanda founded The Empowerment Studio, a dynamic space for women to connect, grow, and share resources. Her work through retreats like **Quiet Girl SZN** and her **Recycle U** workshops reflects her dedication to helping women break free from past hurts and step into lives filled with purpose and joy.

Towanda believes that every woman has the power to live the life she was meant to live. Her message throughout this devotional and beyond is clear: healing, transformation, and empowerment are within reach for every woman who is willing to quiet the noise of life and listen for God's voice.

To learn more about Towanda and her work, visit **www.aliferecycled.com** and explore the transformational opportunities waiting for you.

www.ingramcontent.com/pod-product-compliance
Lightning Source LLC
Chambersburg PA
CBHW062006180426